Politics and  1835–1850

BISHOP AUCKLAND COLLEG
LEARNING RESOURCE LIBRARY
ACCESSION NO. 203098
CLASS NO. 320.942

Collins New Advanced History Series

Politics and the People 1835-1850

K H Randell

COLLINS
EDUCATIONAL

General Editors
K H Randell   J W Hunt

© K H Randell 1972

Printed in Great Britain
Collins Clear Type Press
Set in Monotype Plantin

ISBN 0 00 327212 5

First published 1972
Reprinted 1987, 1988

Conditions of sale: This book is sold subject to the condition that it shall not, by way of trade or otherwise, be lent, re-sold, hired out or otherwise circulated without the publisher's prior consent in any form of binding or cover other than that in which it is published and without a similar condition including this condition being imposed on the subsequent purchaser.

Contents

Editors' Foreword

The series of which this book is a part is designed to meet the needs of students in Sixth Forms and those taking courses in further and higher education. In assessing these needs two factors especially have been taken into account: the limits on the student's time which preclude the reading of all the important scholarly works, and the importance of providing stimulus to thought and imagination. Therefore the series, which has considerably more space available than even the larger single-volume textbooks on the period, presents the interpretations which have altered or increased our understanding of the age, as well as including sufficient detail to illustrate and enliven the subject. Most important of all, emphasis has been placed on discussion. Instead of outlining supposedly established facts, problems are posed as they were faced by the people of the time and as they confront the historian today in his task of interpretation. The student is thus enabled to approach the subject in an attitude of enquiry, and is encouraged to exercise his own mind on the arguments, never closed, of historiography. In so doing he will gain some knowledge of the methods of historians and of the kinds of evidence they use. He should also find enjoyment by the way.

The arrangement of the series, with several volumes covering particular aspects over a long period, and others with more strict chronological limits, has enabled each author to concentrate on an area of special interest, and should make for flexibility in use by the reader.

K.H.R.
J.W.H.

Full details of historical works referred to in the text will be found in the list of Further Reading on page 125. Only where the work is not included is a full reference given in the text.

Chapter I

Chartism

1 The problem It is significant that in the mid 1830s 'working classes', rather than 'working class', was the term used to describe the great mass of the population which, in social and economic status, fell below the level of the middle class, for it was not a homogeneous group. At one end of the scale were those skilled workers such as the engine-builders and printers who often found that the demand for their labour exceeded the supply—a situation conducive to high wage rates. These men were able to surround themselves with luxuries that most of their fellow workers had never enjoyed: soundly constructed and maintained houses, with a room set aside for 'best' and furnished in the latest style; books other than those that might have been handed down from generation to generation; respectable clothes in which to copy the public activities of their betters on high days and holidays; and cash savings for the rainy day that came sometimes even to them. For these skilled workers, in normal times, economic grievances hardly existed.

The same could not be said of the handloom weavers, block printers, framework knitters and other groups who made up the lower end of the scale, for these people suffered hardship even in good years. The weaving and printing of cloth were increasingly being done on power-driven machines which could produce much more cheaply than could their hand-operated rivals. As a result the wages of the hand workers had to be reduced frequently if their goods were to find a market. To make matters worse, there were far too many weavers who wanted work, for there was a steady, though undramatic, influx of Irishmen, especially into Lancashire, many of whom took up weaving when they could find no other employment. A similar situation existed in the East Midlands, where many people were employed in making stockings and hose on knitting frames. Here anybody who was short of money could hire a frame and enter the trade. Competition for work made it easier for employers to reduce wages, especially when they were finding it hard to sell their goods. These, the lowest paid of industrial workers, received between a third and a half of the wages earned by the average male worker. Even when they worked for sixty or seventy hours in a week they could not earn more than enough to keep themselves and their families alive. So they lived and worked in a dwelling that was likely to be dilapidated, sparsely furnished, almost devoid of possessions of a personal nature, and heated only spasmodically during the winter. They ate mainly bread or potatoes, counting bacon ends, cheese and fat as frequent, but by no means regular, extras. On the day before they received their pay they tended to go without. Their clothes were seldom more than rags and for replacements they often relied on charity. On top of all these hardships they had to live with the knowledge that things could only get worse, for experience had taught them that they did not get better.

Between the two extremes came the majority of workers, who, when times were good, earned enough to rent a four-roomed cottage, eat meat several days a week, buy clothes and boots when the old ones wore out, and drink several pints of beer on a Saturday night after being paid. Yet for many there was much to complain about. In order to obtain wages that allowed the purchase of more than the bare necessities of life, long hours had to be worked. For five days in each week there was little more to life than work and sleep, and on the sixth day work would continue until the late afternoon. Working conditions were often most disagreeable. Most publicity was given to the plight of the women and children in the mines, but the men suffered just as much and were more likely to be injured in one of the frequent explosions. Iron and steel producers and gas workers had to endure excessive heat and fumes which frequently led to fatal lung diseases. Although few were forced to work at the rate of the experienced railway navvy, most had to keep up a speed which left them with little energy when their day's labour was done. The tiny minority who went on to evening classes at the Mechanics' Institute must have had iron constitutions.

For most of the working classes times were relatively good in the years before 1836. Then followed six years of almost unbroken gloom. The already despairing outworker in one of the decaying industries was tried to the limits of his endurance, while even the skilled worker was made to feel the helplessness and insecurity of his position. When things were at their worst there was unemployment. Factories and mines closed, and employers no longer supplied the weavers and nailers with the yarn and wire that they needed to carry out their crafts in their own homes. Work in any one industry, however, hardly ever came to a complete standstill. Much more frequent was the phenomenon of short time, with factories only opening two or three days each week, or masters giving their outworkers only sufficient materials for a few hours' work. Just as regular a feature of bad times was the reduction of wages. Those in factories would find their incomes cut by ten or twenty per cent, while domestic workers, paid by the amount they produced, often suffered a bigger cut in their piece rate. The trouble was all the worse because it coincided with a series of poor grain harvests in this country. Wheat, which had stood at 39/- a quarter in 1835, cost over 70/- four years later. The worker found that food was becoming more expensive just as his income was falling.

The resulting hardships were suffered unequally by the different classes of workers, but all found themselves, for a period at least, very badly off. For the lucky ones it was only a matter of drawing out savings so that the normal standard of living could be maintained through a period of underemployment. For more it was a question of pawning, or even selling, prized possessions to buy food. For the poorest it entailed the sale of all possessions, including bedding and cooking utensils, and a gnawing hunger, even after eating the scraps of bread that composed their meals for days on end. Few are recorded as having starved to death but many came close to it, and more died as a result of illnesses made fatal by their weakened resistance. It is hardly surprising that those who suffered most came to look upon life—both their own and that of others—as an expendable commodity, for death was never far away. Membership of a burial club was felt to be a necessity.

There was, in fact, no need for anybody to starve to death. Since the reign of the first Elizabeth a Poor Law system had existed to help those unable to support themselves. Lower-paid workers, in town as well as country, had grown used to supplementing their meagre incomes from this source whenever food prices were high or wages low. They were therefore horrified when they heard, often in a garbled version, the terms of the 1834 Poor Law Amendment Act*. It seemed that what they had come to regard as a right was to be taken away from them, for relief was only to be given to those prepared to enter a workhouse. This would mean that those who were unprepared to sacrifice all self-esteem by seeking admission to one of the new 'bastilles' would have to endure even greater hardships than usual. Little effort was made to implement the new system in the industrial areas until 1836, but a worse time could hardly have been chosen, for now the most vulnerable of the working classes were simultaneously stricken by declining wages, rising prices and the abolition of outdoor relief. Never was the condition of the poorer workers more wretched.

2 The ideal solution   Before the emergence of Chartism a large number of the labouring classes saw in the trade unions a hope of immediate and real improvement in their conditions. From 1824, when the restrictions imposed by the Combination

* See J. W. Hunt, *Reaction and Reform 1815-1841* in this series

Laws were repealed*, more and more workers joined organisations which promised to solve their problems through industrial action. By 1833, when the Grand National Consolidated Trade Union (G.N.C.T.U.) flashed comet-like across the sky, more than one million men were enrolled. Thereafter numbers declined, although for how long has yet to be established.

Those who put their trust in trade unions did so in the hope that they could thereby resist any reduction in wage levels. If they hoped for a wage increase it was normally for the restoration of a rate that had existed in the not too distant past. Few seriously imagined that by combining together they would be able to extract from employers higher wages than had ever been paid before. Less dramatic, but hardly less important to men who seldom lacked necessities, were the efforts made by organised labour to remove other causes of hardship: the withholding of wages to outworkers on the pretext that the employer must first dispose of the goods; the partial payment of wages by means of tokens which could only be spent at specified and therefore expensive shops; the fining of workers for minor, and often fabricated, breaches of regulations, especially with regard to standards of workmanship; and the high rents charged by many employers for both tools and work space.

That the working classes should have concentrated their efforts on easing by direct methods the pressure of higher prices and lower wages is hardly surprising. Nor is it to be wondered at that such an immediate problem as overlong working hours should have been approached in the same way. In this case, however, the basis of activity was not usually small local groups as it was with trade unionism both before and after the brief flirtation with the idea of national unions. Instead, meetings attended by thousands of workers were organised where speeches were given and resolutions passed in favour of shorter hours. The aim was not to influence local employers but to persuade Parliament to pass a law making it illegal for factories to operate

* See J. W. Hunt, *Reaction and Reform 1815-1841* in this series

for more than ten hours a day. There was no concerted plan behind this movement, but in Joseph Rayner Stephens there was a leader who knew how to inflame passions by dwelling on the wrongs of the poor. As a former Methodist preacher his approach was religious, and he regularly invoked the wrath of God on those who oppressed the weak. His suggestions that God would not be displeased if the property of employers was to be consumed by fire struck a chord in 'a generation accustomed to violent talk and craving for dramatic leadership'.

This agitation did not completely die away until the passage of the Ten Hours Act in 1847, but more generally than trade unionism it was taken over by later movements. The first of these was also aimed at the removal by legislation of a particular evil—the Poor Law Amendment Act of 1834. When the agitation started in 1836, the New Poor Law had hardly made an appearance in East Lancashire or the West Riding of Yorkshire, where both the short-time and anti-Poor Law movements chiefly flourished. What moved so many to display their opposition to the new law by attending mass meetings was fear rather than the reality of the new system. The prospect of confinement in one of the new Poor Law bastilles was much more disturbing than actual entry could ever have been, for rumours of the intended massacring of the poor within them not only circulated but were widely believed. Once again Stephens was on hand to increase both fear and the determination to resist, and in this he was joined by Richard Oastler, the chief organiser in the West Riding, and John Fielden, one of the few factory owners to campaign for greater governmental control over industrial conditions. Both men had also been prominent in the short-time movement.

Success for the trade union, ten-hours or anti-Poor Law movements would have resulted in the immediate alleviation of mental and physical suffering, but it would have left the structure of social, economic and political life unaltered. Many 'friends of the people' believed that only a solution which brought about fundamental changes would be satisfactory. Such was the programme of the G.N.C.T.U., and some hoped that such a union would be able to organise a National Holiday, or general strike, which would result in the representatives of the workers replacing Parliament as the governing body of the nation. Only from such a workers' assembly, they believed, could the desired changes in the law be secured. Equally radical were Robert Owen, the instigator of the G.N.C.T.U., and the many self-educated workers who supported him in his plans for co-operation. They aimed at nothing less than a social and economic revolution, in which capitalism would be destroyed and all those who lived on rents, profits and interest made to work for a living. Thus the leisured classes would disappear and the money that had previously paid for their luxury would be shared amongst the producers, and raise the standard of living of the majority. This was to be brought about by workers co-operating in production, instead of selling their labour to an employer who pocketed much of the wealth they created and used it to satisfy his own desires. While it is difficult to hold such a view of the employer today, when many firms have become public companies and the boss is himself the paid representative of an army of faceless shareholders, in the 1830s nearly every employer was known by name and sight, was living in close contact with his workers, and might be seen to be spending large sums of money on personal gratification while dependents of employees declined or died through lack of proper nourishment.

It has often been stated that the trade union, short-time, anti-Poor Law and co-operative movements 'gave rise' to Chartism. If by this it is meant that without the earlier agitations Chartism would not have come into existence, the claim is highly dubious. Chartism arose from 'bitter discontent grown fierce and mad'. Its origins lay in the appalling living and working conditions suffered by the majority of the population; it developed out of the short-time and anti-Poor Law movements only in the sense that it followed hard on their heels and that many leaders and supporters were common to both. But the initiatives that launched Chartism came from elsewhere and doubtless would have been forthcoming irrespective of other movements. Yet Chartism gained in important ways from the work of its forerunners. Not only were there multitudes of people in the North who had been stirred up and made receptive to new ideas, but a newspaper, the *Northern Star*, which was to become the movement's chief organ of propaganda, attaining sales of 50,000 per week in early 1839, had been founded at Leeds in 1837 by Feargus O'Connor, whose failure to rival Daniel O'Connell as an Irish leader had caused him to seek in England the power he craved. Of greatest importance, however, was the fact that many solutions had been tried and all had failed. Without this the degree of unity that Chartism achieved would have been unthinkable, for rival agitations would have been started as each setback occurred. Chartism's claim to be the only hope remaining to the working classes was largely responsible for its surprisingly long life.

The solution offered by Chartism was, on the face of it, purely political. The People's Charter, drawn up in May 1838 by William Lovett, a cabinet-maker and Secretary of the London Working Men's Association, described in detail a radical democratic system which it was hoped would soon become law. At its heart lay the famous six points which were to become to many the hallmark of the movement, despite the fact that the six were of greatly varying significance and in no way sacrosanct: not all were included in each of the three petitions to Parliament, and Carlyle, writing in 1839 and 1843, took it for granted that there were only five points in the Charter.

None of the points was entirely new and most could be traced back, through the campaigns of 'Orator' Hunt, William Cobbett and Major Cartwright*, to both the English Jacobins of the 1790s and the Radicals who had championed the cause of 'Wilkes and Liberty' in the 1760s. This was especially true of universal male suffrage, whose supporters even claimed for it a pedigree stretching back to the mid-seventeenth century. Not so, of course, of votes for women, which it had at first been intended to include in the Charter, but which had been dis-

* *See* J. W. Hunt, *Reaction and Reform 1815-1841* in this series

carded as impracticable. Many regarded the situation in which most of those who paid taxes and obeyed laws had no say in choosing the assembly that prescribed them, as an abuse well worthy of correction for its own sake. Others saw that the right to vote was in itself irrelevant unless the voter could freely and frequently exercise his right to elect anybody he might choose, and unless his vote was of equal value to that of all other citizens. Thus the other five points followed logically from the first.

The demand for a secret ballot was of long standing and arose from the belief that many electors voted as they did through fear of the consequences if they did otherwise. Although it is impossible to say how often a tenant voted for his landlord's candidate through a sense of duty, and how often through fear of eviction or displeasure, it is clear that open voting led to unfair pressures being applied. For many, a vote could only be genuinely free if it were secret.

The law that required M.P.s to be in possession of a landed estate of a minimum annual value was ignored in many cases, but could always be called upon by a man's enemies, as Feargus O'Connor found to his cost in 1835 when his election to the House of Commons was declared invalid. Until it was removed a free choice of candidates could not be secured. Equally important in this respect was the payment of M.P.s, for without it few working men could afford to sit in Parliament. Less important (it was not one of the six points) was the provision for the expenses of each election to be met by a specially levied local rate, thus further reducing the financial demand made upon candidates.

The Septennial Act of 1716 had laid down that a fresh parliament must be summoned at least every seven years. Such was the law when the Chartists put forward their demands for annual parliaments, which, it was felt, would give the voter the greatest possible control over his representatives. That votes should be of equal value was to be ensured by having three hundred constituencies, whose boundaries would be changed after every census so that the number of voters in each would be as nearly as possible the same.

The cynic has for long said that it is only the rich who can afford to have principles. Certainly, many of those who came to call themselves Chartists were not motivated by abstract notions of political justice, as were the aristocratic Radicals of earlier generations. They believed that democracy was not an end in itself, but rather a means of achieving an end—'the economic and social regeneration of society'. One has only to read the reported speeches of leading Chartists in order to realise that there was little agreement on the ways in which society was to be regenerated. One suspects that the majority of the uneducated and politically naive rank and file supporters were with Stephens and O'Connor when they promised, in their more unguarded moments, that once the Charter became law every worker would be well clothed, well housed and well fed, with 'roast beef, plum pudding and strong beer', in return for a few hours work each day. Their vision of the new England hardly differed from the Viking's idea of Valhalla, where the feasting never stopped. O'Connor told the Commons in 1848 that 'he was ready, if he had the Charter granted tomorrow, to put every man willing to labour to work, and to earn double and treble the wages he now earned'. It is hardly surprising that simple working folk did not demand proof that such a change was possible; they believed that government could do anything and that their desires could be fulfilled.

A similar, but less extreme, position was taken up by those thoughtful souls who were motivated by a sense of justice rather than greed. 'A fair day's wage for a fair day's work' was a demand frequently made by Chartist orators and it was as frequently applauded by working class audiences. 'Fair' could, of course, be defined in many ways, but at its least demanding it required a positive answer to what Harriet Martineau called 'the question whether the toil of life is not to provide a sufficiency of bread'. Others, more graphically, requested conditions that were at least as good as those under which the black slaves of America lived. More positively, some claimed that a fair wage must equal the amount of wealth that a worker created. This, in its turn, implied that the employer deserved little and the idle rich nothing. Printed at the bottom of the membership cards of each of the working men's associations was the maxim, 'The man who evades his share of useful labour diminishes the public stock of wealth, and throws his burden upon his neighbour', a clear statement of what was regarded as the parasitical nature of the capitalist class. In a similar vein O'Connor asked one audience, 'Why should you not have institutions to make these people get their living honestly?'

The National Debt was a source of great annoyance to the large numbers of self-educated workers who came into contact with the principles of political economy through the newspapers and books they saw in their local reading room. They felt that those who owned the debt, the fundholders, were living in luxury at the expense of the productive classes in society, for the interest on the debt was paid from taxation. That the debt had largely been incurred in conducting what was regarded as a class war, waged by the aristocracy of England on the common people of France, made the situation even more vexatious. Some Chartists advocated the repudiation of this gigantic burden and a drastic lowering of taxation, which was felt to be excessively heavy, especially on the necessities of life. A minority, with one eye on their possible sympathisers amongst the property-owning classes, merely desired a lowering of the existing rate of interest, and a few, mostly close associates of Thomas Attwood in Birmingham, claimed that an inflationary note-issuing policy should be adopted to reduce the real value of fundholders' property.

Because of the rivalry between Chartism and the Anti-Corn Law League the impression that the Chartists were opposed to the repeal of the Corn Laws has become widespread. O'Connor, it is true, believed that such a change in the law would have an adverse effect on the labouring classes, for he presumed that it would lead to falling prices and a consequent enhancement of the value of the National Debt and thus of the burden of tax imposed on the poor. He also thought that if repeal should, as many of its opponents suggested, spell the ruin of British agriculture, a flood of unemployed workers would descend on the towns, adding to the already overstocked labour market and forcing down wage rates. At the same time the reduction in rural purchasing power would result in a lower demand for manufactured goods. The majority of Chartist speakers, however, declared against the hated bread tax, as had most popular orators since Waterloo. They did not quarrel with the Anti-Corn Law League over aims but rather over priorities. They considered that repeal could not, or in some cases should not, be obtained until a parliamentary democracy had been established. Some were even prepared to see in the repeal agitation a cunning plot hatched by the ruling classes to deflect the will of the voteless masses into less harmful channels. Others feared a repetition of 1832, when the middle class, backed by the lower orders, had gained what they wanted but had refused to give their allies their share of the prize. Thus they were hostile to the Anti-Corn Law League because its solution, though not harmful, was a middle-class one, and as such irrelevant.

The anti-Poor Law and short-time movements, which had provided such fertile soil for the Charter, retained sufficient support for the implementation of their aims by legislative action to become a stock-in-trade promise of Chartist leaders. Equally common was the stated intention to abolish the 'despotic' police forces which were sprouting up in many places in the wake of the hated Metropolitan 'bobbies'. Given the experience of post-revolutionary Europe as well as a number of well-publicised police 'atrocities' in Britain, it is hardly surprising that the working man should see the new-style constable as a threat to his life and liberty.

3 Ways and means The leading lights of the London Working Men's Association (William Lovett, Henry Hetherington, John Cleave and James Watson), whose discussions resulted in the Charter, took it for granted that they would work within the existing constitutional framework, gaining concessions by persuasion rather than force. Their experiences during the previous decade had convinced them that although it might be necessary, as with the agitation against the 4d. newspaper duty, to ignore unjust laws, violence was never necessary, for the good cause always triumphed in the end. They had been impressed by the power of public opinion and saw in it the means of fulfilling their desires. Therefore they thought of themselves as propagandists, setting out to prove that the present political system was unjust and that those at present unworthy of the vote would quickly be made worthy by experience in using it. They attempted to educate the political classes by issuing pamphlets which argued their case, and the excluded classes by encouraging them to meet together and seriously discuss matters of political and moral importance. At first they had no hope of rapid success, but the events of 1838 and early 1839 convinced them that they had been too pessimistic and made them forget their gradualist ideas; they were carried away by the excitement of the times.

Thomas Attwood and the other leaders of the reawakened Birmingham Political Union were responsible for suggesting that a National Petition in favour of a further reform of Parliament should be organised. It was the marriage of the Charter with the petition in 1838 which marked the beginning of Chartism as a popular movement. The Birmingham leaders, who unlike their London counterparts were mainly middle-class, had played a leading part in the reform agitation of 1830-2*, and they naturally believed that a similar agitation would lead to a similarly successful outcome. They had learnt by experience that Parliament would yield once it was clear that a majority in the country favoured a measure, and their agitation was aimed at proving just that. They looked upon violence as being irrelevant to their cause.

Soon, however, events strengthened the position of those who prided themselves on being realists, knowledgeable in life's game, where to be strong was to be victorious. As Parliament showed itself unimpressed by the mere numbers in support of a cause, the argument that force was an essential weapon became more convincing. The majority of realists reasoned in

* See J. W. Hunt, *Reaction and Reform 1815-1841* in this series

21

a way that has become so common in international affairs since 1945—that those who possess a large offensive capability will never need to use it, as potential enemies will always be prepared, in the last resort, to give way rather than risk devastation. Chartists such as Feargus O'Connor conducted the movement in the early years in such a way as to persuade the governing classes that unless they accepted change they would become the victims of fire and sword. They believed the threat of violence would be sufficient.

The Chartist movement, like most that work for political or social change, tended to attract extremists. There were some people in early Victorian England who wished to re-enact the Jacobin terror of 1794-5 in their own country, and many of these associated themselves with Chartism. One is tempted to look upon them as bloodthirsty villains who enjoyed violence for its own sake, and undoubtedly there were some who thrilled at the thought of sticking their knives into the stomachs of bloated aristocrats. Others, however, cared greatly about the sufferings and injustices of the poor and believed that only swift and violent revolution would save them from starvation. Such men were saddened by what they felt was the lesser of two evils.

'Moral force' and 'physical force' are labels that have been attached to Chartists ever since 1838, and there is hardly a book dealing with the subject that does not use them. Nineteenth-century authors gave the impression that the movement was rigidly divided on this basis, and left no one in doubt that the former were good and the latter bad. More recently this simple analysis has been questioned. It used to be customary to assign Lovett to the 'moral force' and O'Connor to the 'physical force' camp. A close investigation of their public utterances reveals some surprisingly provocative statements by Lovett and much temporising talk by O'Connor. In fact, each could, at different times, be classed as belonging to either group. The same could be said of most of the moderate Chartists. This does not mean, however, that the labels are meaningless. There were undoubtedly deep rifts caused by the question of violence, and men behaved as if committed to one side or the other. One cannot understand the public feuding of the leaders without realising that this was so. But the labels must be used with discretion, for there is no simple scale against which each man may be measured.

The frightened rich in the areas where Chartist activity was greatest were sure that the reformers were 'physical force' supporters to a man. The letters of terrified urban J.P.s, preserved amongst Home Office papers, show that fear of an armed uprising was widespread and that all Chartists were being tarred with the violence brush. Historians have tended to paint a very different picture. Those in sympathy with the aims of Chartism have normally attempted to make the movement respectable by stressing the part played by 'moral force' men. In this they have been encouraged by the large collection of papers compiled by Francis Place*, a London Radical who, wrongly it seems, claimed to have helped draw up the People's Charter. The papers, housed in the British Museum, contain a large amount of evidence about the London Working Men's Association and those who had to do with it, and historians working from these have tended to see the 'moral force' men as more important than they really were. This phenomenon has been accentuated by the fact that few scholars hostile to the aims of the Chartist movement have written about it, for in this country historians usually choose to write on subjects with which they are in sympathy. As a result the impression of moral force neatly balancing physical force has become widespread. Although the truth can never be known, it is very possible that the majority of rank-and-file Chartists, meeting violence in their everyday lives, looked upon it as a natural weapon, to be used whenever the danger of retribution was not too immediate. It was only the minority, blessed with superior wisdom or moral fervour, that was prepared to discountenance what could have been the trump card of the masses.

* See J. W. Hunt, *Reaction and Reform 1815-1841* in this series

With the movement so divided, it is surprising that it found such unity of method as it did. There was, in 1838, general agreement among Chartists that the first step in their campaign should be to petition Parliament to grant the Charter, and in this even such physical force stalwarts as George Julian Harney concurred. Such men believed petitioning would have no effect on Parliament, but they were prepared to go through the motions, feeling that until peaceful methods had proved unsuccessful, armed insurrection would never be sufficiently widely supported. The majority, however, had no doubts about the efficacy of a giant petition, for as Lovett asked, 'How can a corrupt government withstand an enlightened people?' Both Attwood and O'Connor were proclaiming in late 1838 and early 1839 that the Charter would be law within a year, and their actions suggest they were as convinced as their listeners.

At various times during 1838 Attwood talked about a petition of two, three, or six million signatures as the key to success. He and the other early leaders were so confident of support on this scale that they did little to ensure that it was forthcoming. They addressed massive meetings near Glasgow, Birmingham, Manchester and Leeds and smaller ones in other heavily populated areas, but did not get on with the humdrum business of setting up an effective organisation to extract signatures from a somewhat apathetic population. They left it to the initiative of local men, but in many localities there was nobody to give a strong lead. The result was a petition that contained only 600,000 signatures on the date that had first been fixed for its presentation to Parliament. It was not good enough for the men of Bath to expose petition sheets in the markets and streets and to send blank sheets to Salisbury in the hope that people would sign. Nor was the leaving of the petition in Ipswich town hall and later in a public house all that was required if massive support was to be registered. In contrast, Anti-Corn Law League employers, when they were preparing a petition, 'asked' their workers to sign as they received their wages.

The Chartists were also united over the suggestion that a 'General Convention of the Industrious Classes' should meet in London to handle the petition once it had been circulated, and all but the most cautious agreed that this People's Parliament should decide what should be done if it were rejected, as seemed increasingly likely once the euphoria inspired by the mass meetings had subsided. There was also a general consensus on what these 'ulterior measures' should be. Exclusive dealing, whereby Chartists only bought from those who sympathized with the cause, was thought to involve no more sacrifice than would the withdrawal of all moneys from banks and savings accounts, a course of action that had also been widely canvassed during the Reform Bill crisis of 1831-2. The suggestion that Chartists should refrain from purchasing commodities which were heavily taxed, especially tobacco and spirits, demanded a considerable amount of self-denial; so did the most 'ulterior' measure, the National Holiday of one month's duration, when no labour would be sold. Disunity, however, always threatened in a convention comprising on the one hand open supporters of revolution and on the other a large group of men who felt that if the Charter could not be obtained by peaceful means it should not be gained at all. Unbridled speech and fiery tempers led to constant squabbles, and a semblance of cohesion was only possible because the more moderate members gradually withdrew from the convention, and because it was possible to support the idea of a general strike for different reasons. It is ironical that the idea of a prolonged strike was finally abandoned as the result of the intervention of Bronterre O'Brien, a physical force leader, not on any moral grounds but because it was felt that nation-wide support could not be aroused.

When the Anti-Corn Law League suffered initial setbacks it rapidly found other activities which it believed would work better. From a direct approach to Parliament it turned its attention to fund-raising, propaganda and electoral work. Chartism was never able to find such wide-ranging and relevant lines of action. Corn Law repealers could plan to raise £100,000 because many of their supporters were in a position to subscribe three- or four-figure amounts. Not many Chartists, however, could afford more than a few pence at any one time, and this meant that an enormous effort would yield only a moderate return. In early 1839 Attwood could talk about raising £100,000, and Lovett in gaol could plan to establish a national system of education costing £256,000 per annum and financed by the 1d. per week subscriptions of all those who had signed the first petition, but attempts at fund-raising on this scale were never seriously made. The hard facts appear in the paltry £1700 that was collected to pay for the convention of 1839, or the £2000 that was subscribed to the Stephens defence fund after his arrest in 1838. It is true that O'Connell in Ireland was able to depend upon a large income from people just as poor as the Chartists, but he had the support in most areas of a Catholic priesthood which knew well how to extract money from its underfed parishioners. Such a network the Chartists were never able to build. One of the results of the failure of 1838-9 was the determination to establish some sort of permanent organisation with a regular income, but although the National Charter Association, set up in July 1840, had within two years spread into 350 localities and acquired 50,000 members, it received contributions from its branches in a very sporadic manner. Few could discern the path to eventual victory in squeezing pennies out of the starving.

The Anti-Corn Law League hoped to build up in Parliament a large minority of M.P.s pledged to repeal. They worked to persuade electors to vote only for such men, and to qualify new electors who would do likewise. They put forward their own candidates wherever they could, or sought promises from candidates representing the established parties. The Chartists did not match these efforts. This was partly because they had a very narrow base from which to work—they had few supporters in Parliament and in any one constituency there was only a minority of electors in their favour—and partly because most of their leaders, at least in the early years, were very class-conscious and refused to accept the support of non-Chartist middle-class radicals. No sizeable group of Chartist M.P.s could have been established without the help of such people, but a hatred of the employer class, coupled with distrust bred of the events of 1830-2, made it dangerous for Chartist leaders to think of a compromise alliance. If they did they were either abandoned by their supporters or hounded by O'Connor, who alone could work with the Radicals and yet retain the adoration of the masses. Thus there seemed to be little point in penetrating Parliament—intimidating it from outside seemed much more practical.

When the general election of 1841 took place most of the leaders of 1838-9 were languishing in gaol. This did not prevent them, however, from suggesting to their followers the line of action that should be pursued. Nobody argued for an all-out effort to secure the election of Chartists, for this would have resulted in total failure. Instead O'Connor and O'Brien propounded their own theories and feuded with one another from a distance. O'Connor, in negative mood, wished the Whigs to be punished for their failure to accept the full programme of the Charter, and so advised his supporters to back up the Tory candidates in all constituencies. This seemed to O'Brien to be an admission of defeat. He dreamed of establishing a democratic system, if need be, while the old undemocratic one was still in being. He urged Chartists to present themselves as candidates and to work to obtain a majority show of hands at the pre-election hustings meeting. Having won this 'election' where every man had a vote they should refuse to take part in the charade of the official election. These true representatives of the people should then come together to form a proper parliament and should demand that Westminster hand over all power to it. It was O'Connor's advice, however, that was generally followed.

During the forties many Chartists came to doubt the wisdom of acting without allies. This softening in attitude made possible forays into the political arena, and in the election of 1847 several Chartists had hopes of being returned to Parliament. Only O'Connor at Nottingham was successful, however, and thus to him went the honour of being the only person ever to be elected as a proclaimed Chartist—that is, if local government be excepted, for in Leeds Chartists determined to have a say in town affairs and in the decade after 1843 seventeen of their number were elected to the borough council. Such an impact, however, was not made elsewhere.

The problem of retaining the allegiance of their followers in the years after their first failures was common to both the Anti-Corn Law League and Chartism. The League tackled this in a centralised way, organising annual large-scale delegates' meetings, setting ambitious fund-raising targets, and maintaining pressure on M.P.s and Parliament alike. They were remarkably successful. Chartism, in contrast, largely depended on the ideas and energies of local leaders and thus was well served in some areas but not in others. Thomas Cooper in Leicester showed remarkable skill in organising social activities for his several thousand followers, and his movement became the focal point in the lives of many men and women. The same was true in many Scottish communities where, in 1840, it was claimed that 'universal suffrage . . . has become a part of the social character of the people. It is associated with their amusements. It has become identified with their religion.' Chartism was, in such areas, fulfilling so many of the functions normally associated with the Church that it is hardly surprising that north of the border and in Birmingham Chartist churches were actually founded. Chartist hymns were sung, Chartist prayers were read, and sermons based on suitable Chartist texts were preached. A similar phenomenon was Teetotal Chartism, which flourished in the West Country under the stimulus of Henry Vincent, although in this case the exhortations to abandon alcoholic beverages seem to have drowned the political appeals.

None of these activities, however, did anything to make the six points law. Only Parliament or a revolution could do that, and the former had refused while the latter was deemed to be impracticable. Thus Chartism could only mark time in the hope that a fresh solution would present itself. None ever did and the movement had to satisfy itself with variations on the petitioning theme. Attwood in 1838 had suggested that petition after petition should be organised until Parliament's will to resist was destroyed. The majority doubted if such a day would ever arrive, and although they were prepared to expend their energies on collecting signatures for the petitions of 1842 and 1848, they hankered after a sledgehammer that would destroy the resistance of Parliament with one blow. Thus, when widespread strikes occurred in Lancashire in the summer of 1842 the temptation to exploit the situation was too great to be resisted. Chartists, rather belatedly, attempted to take control of the movement and turn it into the National Holiday that had been so dear to their hearts three years earlier. At strikers' meetings resolutions stating that 'all labour should cease until the People's Charter became the law of the land' were piloted through, and Chartists with physical force sympathies believed once again that their hour was at hand. Another road to rapid victory was planned in conjunction with the 1848 petition. Chartists in their hundreds of thousands were to gather at Kennington Common, to the south of London, and to march on Westminster to present their millions of gathered signatures to what it was hoped would be a terrified and amenable Parliament. They believed that nobody would be prepared to deny the demands of the desperate crowds that stood before them. In fact the crowds did not materialise and the march did not take place.

4 The course of events The career of a politician has a certain beginning and a certain end, and even the Anti-Corn Law League was founded on one day and dissolved on another. The story of Chartism is not so simple. Hovell considered that the Birmingham meeting of 6 August 1838 marked the 'official beginning of the Chartist movement' because there, for the first time, the leaders of the Midlands, North, Scotland and London appeared together in support of the Charter. But to accept this date, or May of the same year when the Charter was produced, would be to exclude an important part of the history of the movement. Briggs contends that 'Chartism was born before the name', and this is true not only because the movement was the continuation of a long tradition of radical agitation but also because much had been done towards gaining support for the ideas of the Charter before the document itself was drawn up. In June 1836 the London Working Men's Association was founded by a group of skilled artisans who had combined together in radical causes during the previous seven years, and one of its declared aims was 'to seek by every legal means to place all classes of society in possession of equal rights'. One of those 'legal means' was to be the establishment of similar associations in all parts of the country, and thanks to the efforts of the three missionaries who were sent out in 1837, there were at least 150 of them by the end of the year. To a lesser extent the men of Birmingham had worked, since the reorganisation of their Political Union in April 1837, to rekindle interest in an ultra-radical political programme in other areas, and especially in Scotland. Thus the agitation was well under way before its name was invented, even if it could not yet boast a massive following.

Between its origination and its effective termination in late 1848, the fortunes of Chartism varied greatly. The impressive growth of the first year was outdone by the blossoming that occurred in 1838, when massive meetings were organised in order to acclaim the Charter, and to elect representatives to attend the Convention. Hopes were high among the tens or even hundreds of thousands who stood or sat all day listening to harangues of considerable length and intensity (two to three hours was not uncommon), for it was presumed that victory was not far distant. As summer turned to autumn the outdoor gatherings assumed a sinister air, for evening meetings had to be held by torchlight. Flickering light of high intensity surrounded by thickest darkness has always been a potent psychological weapon, and the Chartists used it to the full, especially in their 'round the town' processions, during which they sent forth 'volleys of the most hideous groans on passing the office of some hostile newspaper, or the house of some obnoxious magistrate or employer' before marching off to hear speeches and pass resolutions. The early part of 1839, with torchlight meetings banned and the Convention in session, saw a decline in activity on the grand scale, but in many areas desperate men armed and drilled themselves in readiness for the struggle they felt sure was soon to come. Mass meetings in Whit week were less well attended than had been expected and those in August, meant as a substitute for the abandoned month's strike, caused little stir. Yet in many a dingy room over a public house plans for an insurrection were laid, although there seems to have been little or no contact between the various groups of plotters. Such activity reached its height at the end of the year, once John Frost had been sentenced to death (later commuted to transportation for life) for his part in the Newport Rising, in which Chartists from the valleys marched on Newport only to be scattered with casualties by a small body of troops, but nothing of note resulted from it. With the petition rejected, the Convention disbanded, and over five hundred leading men in gaol, the prospects at the start of the new decade were not at all good. It is little wonder, therefore, that optimists of the ruling class thought that Chartism had failed.

A recovery began in July 1840 when twenty-three delegates, mainly from the North, met together in Manchester and decided to form a National Charter Association so that the movement could be provided with a formal organisation. The Association flourished, and after a slow beginning many local groups —often former Working Men's Associations, Political Unions or even trade union branches—transformed themselves into localities. The greatest growth came in the first four months of 1842 when, it was claimed, about seventy new localities were added to the 282 already in existence, and membership increased by an even greater proportion. The new body decided, in September 1841, to collect signatures for a new petition, and when the time came for it to be presented to the House of Commons in the following April, the six-mile-long roll of paper containing 3,317,702 signatures had to be broken up before it could be manoeuvred into the Chamber. When the Commons failed to be impressed, the Convention that had once again been elected could think of no suitable action and so contented itself with pouring forth abuse.

Before this occurred, however, it had become clear that all was not well. Lovett and Collins, the Birmingham working men's leader, had made plans while in prison together, and on their release in 1841 they had proclaimed to the world their proposal that Chartism should be transformed into an educational organisation, aiming to make the common man fit for the vote. Despite the fact that O'Connor's raging denunciation of the plan led to the unseemly withdrawal of most of the promises of support that the scheme had already received, damage had been done and many moderate Chartists withdrew from the movement in disgust at O'Connor's outbursts. A potentially more dangerous split threatened as a result of the decision by Joseph Sturge—a rich Birmingham Quaker and a member of the Anti-Corn Law League—to start a Complete Suffrage Union in order to unite all classes in the struggle for moderate parliamentary reform, for a large number of Chartists, tired either of O'Connor or of physical force talk, immediately gave their support to it. With travelling lecturers like Henry Vincent, who had earlier been responsible for the establishment of many Working Men's Associations and for the spread of Chartism into South Wales, the new movement quickly established itself in many areas, and was even able to compete effectively with the National Charter Association in petitioning in 1842. O'Connor saw in it an extreme threat to the future of Chartism, for it represented compromise, which had often proved fatal to movements seeking revolutionary change. Cobden had battled against the acceptance of anything but the total and immediate repeal of the Corn Laws, and his counterpart in Chartism was equally determined to prevent a 'sell out'. His denunciations of O'Brien and the other prominent Chartists associated with Sturge were violent in the extreme, for he hated them as traitors to the cause. When the Complete Suffrage Union held its first conference in Birmingham in April 1842 O'Connor organised a Chartist conference to force all reformers to declare openly where their loyalties lay.

When the Complete Suffrage Union decided to adopt the six points of the Charter, O'Connor no longer had good grounds for opposition. By remaining committed to the destruction of the 'New Move' he did Chartism a great disservice, for when the second conference, of December 1842, which was well attended by O'Connor's supporters, was broken up by the withdrawal of the middle-class elements who refused to accept a vote in favour of retaining the name of the Charter, all hope of a united radical movement was lost. It was understandable that those who had worked for five years in the cause should have been annoyed that newcomers wished to start a new organisation rather than join the old one, but it is impossible to discount the suggestion that O'Connor wanted to retain the pre-eminent position he had by then established.

Before Sturge's attempts to unite reformers of all classes had been wrecked on the rocks of pride and ambition, the image of Chartism had been further tarnished by its connection with the Plug Plot of mid-1842. Widespread strikes (forced on some workers by the removal of the plugs from the boilers used to produce steam for factory engines) in Lancashire and Staffordshire were kept going by Chartist agitators, with the blessing of a hastily convened executive committee, and ended in considerable rioting and the arrest of more than 1500 people. The effect upon public opinion was considerable, for Chartism and unreasonable violence once more became linked in the minds of the propertied classes, who believed in logic and tranquillity. 1842 was indeed the second year of setbacks for the Chartist cause.

On this occasion, however, reverses were not to be followed by a marked recovery. In part this was due to the fact that as the economic climate improved, prices and unemployment, and with them, hardship, were diminished. Many who now lost the spur of hunger had already lost faith and hope in Chartism and were easy victims of apathy or the allurements of other causes. Only the efforts of O'Connor, who in September 1843 gained complete control of the National Charter Association, sustained the movement. He toured the country, with little regard for his own health and comfort, addressing meetings of all sizes in all types of places, and undoubtedly provoked renewed determination in many who had previously wavered. He had always been the most popular of the Chartist leaders, with his massive frame and booming voice (a fine vehicle for the outpourings of vituperation and wit alike), and his flair for a gesture that would endear him to simple folk, but now he secured a place for himself in the hearts of the loyal the like of which had never been known. Proud, boastful, thoughtless, quick to anger, and at times selfish he may have been, but his great-heartedness somehow outweighs all those faults, and demands for him recognition as a great 'friend of the people'. From 1845 to 1848 his efforts were mainly directed towards establishing his Chartist Land Scheme, which critics have considered to have been more diversionary than the Educational, Church and Teetotal Chartisms that he so vehemently attacked. His idea was to raise funds in the form of shares from among Chartists and to buy land that would be distributed in plots of up to four acres to some of the shareholders. Three estates were established, but the idea, relying as it did on the merits of intensive spade husbandry, was not a good one and even if financially sound would never have achieved very much. It seems unfair, however, to argue that the land scheme, by disillusioning many supporters, was responsible for the relatively poor response to the events of 1848. It is more likely that the scheme, in many places, kept alive an organisational framework which could be reactivated when conditions were more appropriate to new agitation.

That time came in 1848, but once again the basic Chartist dilemma was apparent: persuasion could not work and force required an intensity of support that was not forthcoming. None the less it is sad that Chartism's final appearance on the national stage should have turned into a farce. A meeting was planned for 10 April on Kennington Common, and it was intended that a procession of several hundred thousand supporters should accompany the petition to Westminster, where its acceptance would be assured by the physical presence of so many of its signatories. In the event, hardly one tenth of the expected gathering materialised—many of those who came being spectators—and O'Connor was persuaded by the police to abandon the march. The petition, when examined by a committee of the House of Commons, was found to have just under two million, rather than the five million seven hundred thousand valid signatures that had been claimed, and this ensured that it was treated with derision. When, several months later, another parliamentary committee pronounced against the legality and efficacy of the land scheme the discomfiture was complete. Although plans for uprisings, similar to those of 1839, were plentiful in the latter part of the year, nothing came of them, and never again was the pulse-rate of the Establishment to be raised by the spectre of a Chartist revolution. O'Connor continued with his efforts, although increasingly handicapped by mental disorders, and was succeeded by the trusty lieutenant of his later years, Ernest Jones, who was finally to bury the movement in the conspiratorial origins of international socialism.

5 The pattern of support In the past the study of local history has generally been looked upon as an occupation suitable for scholarly members of the clergy and graduates researching for a second degree, but not for hardened professionals, who would be wasted on anything less than national history. Happily this attitude is rapidly dying, and as it does so our knowledge of Chartism increases. There is, of course, a place for a single-volume national history of Chartism (especially as a major one has not been produced for fifty years), but equally important are thorough local studies of the movement, for regional variations were so great that most generalisations about Chartism mislead as much as they guide. *Chartist Studies*, with its seven essays on individual areas, gave a fine start, and work on other areas has since been published, but much remains to be done before anything like a full picture can be presented. Of particular significance will be enquiries which attempt to discover local variations in the social composition of Chartism and to explain why the agitation flourished in some areas while it rarely appeared in others.

Chartism used to be viewed as a reaction against the Industrial Revolution, and its supporters were thought to be mainly drawn from those groups which were suffering most from the vast economic changes that were taking place. Handloom weavers who were facing increasing competition from power looms, and factory operatives who were subjected to harsh new disciplines were seen as particularly typical. Although it is clear that the 100,000 handloom weavers and the 250,000 adult factory workers featured frequently in the annals of Chartism, it is now obvious that other occupational groupings were just as important. The part played by the hosiery workers of the Leicester area is now appreciated, and an awareness of the importance of such groups as nail makers and coal miners is growing. As this happens the significance of the Industrial Revolution grows less, for in many trades reduced wages were produced by a fall in demand and a rise in the labour supply, rather than by the introduction of machines.

Skilled artisans have traditionally been viewed as the second pillar of Chartist support, largely on the basis of the composition of the London Working Men's Association, about which so much is known. Recent research, while confirming their importance, has revealed the need for a more subtle analysis, as skilled artisans can no longer be said to have formed a homogeneous group. The 'aristocracy of labour', made up of the members of highly paid and secure trades, while dominating the London Working Men's Association, seems generally to have remained aloof from Chartism. Other groups of artisans such as shoemakers, tailors, carpenters and masons, were much more prominent than their richer fellows and provided the leadership in many localities. It is in doubt, however, whether all of them can fairly be classed as skilled, for during the early decades of the nineteenth century large numbers of interlopers, who had served no apprenticeship and whose talents were very limited, had entered such trades and were being used as sweated labour by unscrupulous employers. In pay and status they were little better off than were the outworkers in the textile industry and should really be classed with them. A researcher, of course, rarely has sufficient evidence to be able to decide whether a named tailor or shoemaker belongs to the ranks of the skilled or the unskilled, and thus is unable to signify his exact social position.

It has frequently been stated that agricultural labourers played little part in Chartism, and yet Miss Martineau, writing in the 1840s, classed them as one of the four types of Chartists. That she was not completely mistaken has been shown by studies of Chartist activity in Suffolk, Somerset and Wiltshire, and in Wales, where considerable evidence of participation by farm workers has been uncovered. Further research will probably confirm that in agricultural areas where it had gained a foothold in the local town Chartism tended to spread into the surrounding villages, and there to gain support from those who worked on the land. It would, of course, be unrealistic to claim for country people a leading role in Chartism, but it would seem that their efforts have been consistently underrated.

Considerable interest has been shown in the geographical distribution of Chartism, and nowadays the old supposition that its support to all intents and purposes came from Lancashire and the West Riding is no longer taken seriously. The massive support given by Newcastle, Carlisle and Glasgow to the north, and by Staffordshire and the East Midlands to the south has led commentators to write instead of the urban and industrial basis of the movement. Yet even within industrial areas support for Chartism varied greatly, and this has prompted Professor Briggs to suggest that the greatest following came from 'old centres of decaying or contracting industry' and 'new or expanding single-industry towns'—a most effective way of describing where the greatest concentrations of Chartists were to be found. As further research is done, however, more and more localities will be added to the list of minor Chartist centres, and it should be possible one day to construct a proper distribution map, perhaps with the aid of statistics compiled from the signatures on the three petitions. During this process our opinions on the importance of various areas will no doubt change, as they recently have with respect to London as a result of the findings of Iorwerth Prothero, who has shown that contrary to the traditional view the metropolis was not insensitive to the cause. Previously historians had generalised from the evidence of 1838-9 without knowledge of the rapid growth of support in 1842.

It is only natural that the distribution of Chartism should be explained in terms of the incidence of discontent. 'Want was the chief feeder of Chartism', and it was strongest where hardship was greatest. But the effect of leadership has been constantly underrated. It is often possible to attribute the irregularities in the pattern to good local organisers or the lack of them. The South Wales coalfield was toured by Vincent and Chartism flourished, while in North Wales the mining areas remained quiet. In the declining woollen cloth town of Trowbridge the movement thrived under good leaders, but in similarly placed Frome not many miles away, politics stagnated. Bristol, after succumbing to the mimicry and emotion of Vincent, lacked the men to nurture the enthusiasm once he had gone away. At Bath, only twelve miles away, a lively agitation was kept up by a band of experienced and respected Radicals. The impact of individuals was everywhere apparent, from work by Stephen Tudgey in the village of Monkton Deverill in Wiltshire to that of Thomas Cooper in Leicester, and in many places a passive acceptance of misery was only transformed into strident demands for reform by the tireless efforts of dedicated enthusiasts. Economic conditions created discontent but organisers made it vocal.

6 Success or failure? That Chartism failed would seem to be a truism, for to be successful an organisation must achieve what it sets out to do, and Chartism patently did not. By the time it declined into insignificance, it had not managed to secure even one of its much vaunted six points. The working classes had no more political power when Chartism died than they had had at the time of its birth. Hovell even argues for a more fundamental failure. He claims that Chartism was never certain of its objectives, for it was unable 'to agree on a single definite social ideal'. Chartists recognised the need of political power as a means to an end but could not discover the end itself. They did not fail to achieve an aim, they failed to have one.

Some historians, however, have been unprepared to accept the verdict of total failure. As much as a hundred years ago it was being pointed out that some of the six points had eventually been carried into law. In 1858 the property qualification for M.P.s was done away with; in 1872 the secret ballot was introduced; in 1885 a redistribution of seats on the basis of equal electoral districts took place; in 1911 M.P.s were paid for the first time; and in 1918 nearly all adult males were at last allowed to vote. Even the sixth point, annual parliaments, was brought a stage nearer in 1911 when the maximum time between elections was reduced from seven years to five. From these facts has developed the argument that Chartism was successful in the end. Unfortunately it is not adequate to show that the demands of the Chartists were eventually implemented: a relationship of cause and effect must be established. This is very difficult to do. It can be claimed that many Chartists continued to support reform movements throughout the fifties and sixties and were in part responsible for the Act of 1867 which brought both an extension of the franchise and a redistribution of seats, and that the Chartists by so well airing the ideas of reform made their eventual acceptance more certain. This, however, is hardly conclusive, especially when it is realised that the parliamentary Radicals of the 1830s supported much of the Chartist programme and probably had a greater impact on later events. The secret ballot had been in the original Whig reform proposals of 1831 and it was supported by 216 M.P.s in 1839; 164 had been for triennial parliaments in 1833; in 1837 the abolition of the property qualification was only defeated by 29 votes; and household suffrage was one of the bases of the Radical creed. It is likely that if any events of the 1830s and 1840s are to be directly linked with later reforms, the work of the middle-class Radicals should have first claim to consideration.

To say that Chartists failed to achieve their aims is not to suggest that there were no beneficial results from their activities.

As early as 1839 Carlyle could write that they had forced all thinking men of the community to ponder on the vital 'condition of England question'. If this was so (and there is much evidence that it was) it was indeed a considerable achievement. Disraeli was not the only one to feel that the England of the time was composed of two nations, one ignorant of the life and sufferings of the other, and while such a situation existed the 'haves' in power could not be expected to legislate to improve the condition of the 'have nots', who possessed no political rights. As a result of the early Chartist campaign the state of the working poor became a subject of national interest. Much was written on the subject, and, in keeping with the new spirit of Benthamite radicalism, much investigation was undertaken. As a result the 1840s were graced by a large number of Acts aimed at removing the environmental ills about which Chartist speakers so violently complained.

Those who wish to detract from the significance of the movement could argue that the social reforms would have been forthcoming even if Chartism had not existed. To bolster their argument they could cite the studies of working-class conditions that had been carried out even before 1838, and the numbers of influential humanitarians who had already taken up the cause of the underprivileged. One suspects, however, that had the feeling not got abroad that unless something was done there would be a destructive revolution, the obstacle of conservative inertia would have been too great for the reformers to overcome. It was the Chartists' contribution to frighten into acquiescence those who were normally at best uninterested in such things. Professor Briggs has, however, suggested that Chartism put off rather than advanced reform. His argument is that violent, or as Carlyle termed it 'delirious', Chartism forced the moderate reformers to identify themselves with an unprogressive government and that subsequently they found it difficult to espouse the cause of reform without feeling that they were somehow inviting revolution.

There can be no doubt that Chartism succeeded in improving the morale of many working people. To the hopeless it gave the possibility of improved conditions, at first in the near, and later in the more distant future; to those who lacked status it gave pride at belonging to a recognisable group, with leaders who praised them for the 'fustian jackets, unshorn chins and blistered hands' which had previously been the mark of their inferiority. It is impossible to measure the quantity or quality of this contribution of Chartism to the mental well-being of its supporters, but that does not make it any less worthy of consideration.

The failure of Chartism to accomplish its declared objectives has been explained in many different ways, but once differences of approach have been discounted, it becomes clear that most commentators agree on the major factors involved. Lack of support was a fatal handicap. Especially significant was the inability to attract a large-scale following among the political classes. If, as moral force men desired, Chartism was to succeed by the reasoned conversion of people, those people had to be the decision-takers—M.P.s and electors. Only in this way could the Charter eventually be voted into law by men who agreed with its proposals. The failure was particularly apparent in the case of M.P.s, for not fifty could be found who would support a further investigation of the petitioners' case in 1839 or 1842. But the middle classes were hardly more forthcoming, for Hovell was able to write that Chartism 'was a purely working-class movement, originating exclusively and drawing its whole following from the industrialised and unpropertied working class which had but recently come into existence'. One may be excused for thinking that this overstates the case, but it is in general a correct conclusion. It could of course have been otherwise, for there existed a large number of radical bourgeois who were, when pressed, prepared to grant the justice of the Chartist case. The middle-class members of the Birmingham Political Union had not taken much persuading in 1838, and the well-attended conference of the Complete Suffrage Union in December 1842 had witnessed numerous respectable men willingly accepting the substance, if not the name, of the Charter. Sympathetic writers have described as tragic the death-wish of Chartism, which not only prevented the movement from winning new middle-class supporters, but also led to the loss of those it already had. The situation was brought about in part by the working-class exclusiveness of the movement, typified by the London Working Men's Association's refusal to welcome non-workers into full membership, and in part by the violent words and actions that were so much a part of Chartist activities. To support a radical political organisation in itself endangered a person's respectability, but to associate with one that seemed bent on unleashing the horrors of civil commotion was to court social disaster. Excepting such remarkable men as Ernest Jones, who by remaining a Chartist turned down a legacy of £2000 p.a., none was prepared to do this. The 'steady shrinkage' of the 1839 Convention was caused by the withdrawal of the scandalised middle-class elements, and their alienation was completed by the Birmingham Riot of 15 July and the Newport Rising of 3 November. Those who had summoned up sufficient courage to return to the cause in the following years were driven to despair by the disturbances of late August and September 1842, which signalled the approaching collapse of the strike movement. It is indeed true that in part Chartism was 'slain by the violence of its supporters'.

Those leaders who relied on the intimidation of Parliament as a method were at first certain that they would be able to mobilise most of the labouring classes in their support. That only a minority were in fact ever real Chartists to some extent explains their failure. Suspicions of the truth first obtruded when the 1839 petition was so poorly signed, for despite the efforts of the Convention's fifteen missionaries it totalled no more than 1,280,000 signatures, a figure that was to be surpassed even by the petition against Peel's increase of the Maynooth grant. O'Brien's reason for wishing to abandon the National Holiday was lack of popular support, and Harney, a physical force man long after his fellows had become less extreme, did not favour using the strikes of 1842 as a revolutionary launching-pad, as he realised how little support would be given by other areas. Even John Frost, the leader of the Newport Rising, seems to have been opposed to the attempt because the rest of the country had not been suitably prepared. And all this was at the moments of Chartism's maximum popularity. It would seem that the mistake was to assume 'that the millions who were to sign the Petition would be effective political warriors instead of what they for the most part were—non-combatants who hoped the Birmingham people would win'. There was a lack of people who were prepared to do more than put their mark on a sheet of paper.

Gammage was bitter with O'Connor for his attacks on the leaders of Christian, Knowledge and Temperance Chartism because he could see no reason why all men of the same principles should follow one policy. Unfortunately for the Chartist cause many people agreed with him, and this resulted in a splintering of the movement into factions, especially after 1842. This disunity not only meant that the full force of Chartism could not be concentrated on one course of action, which in itself was very serious, but also led to a steady falling away of support, which had an increasingly debilitating effect. Not only were such national leaders as Attwood, Lovett, O'Brien and Vincent lost to the cause because of internal squabbles, and such local organisers as Cooper of Leicester and Phelp of Bath driven from the fold, but an unnumbered host of the rank and file were given good reason to lose faith in the movement and to withdraw from public life or join the less divided Anti-Corn Law League. How many of these would in any case have ceased to be Chartists for other reasons cannot be guessed. Certainly they would have had to be staunch supporters to endure continuing failure for more than ten years and to retain their enthusiasm through periods of economic boom. In 1845 O'Connor claimed that his greatest success was the creation of an organisation that could withstand 'a long and continuous calm—the greatest danger that can threaten a politician'. In fact Chartism survived rather than withstood the good years of 1842-5, and in the end it was loss of support due to improved wages, lessening unemployment and improved environment that largely killed it. Cobbett had defied people 'to agitate a fellow with a full stomach', and Chartism could not successfully take up the challenge. But not only did the material conditions of the workers improve; their mental condition also took a turn for the better. 'The two nations drew more closely together and sullen hostility gave way to admiration and imitation.' During the 1850s the lower orders began to realise that their own efforts could raise them to the status of their superiors. They increasingly abandoned ideas of replacing the system in favour of striving to move up within it. The revolution that was to bring them an increasingly higher standard of living had taken place, unnoticed, while they struggled unsuccessfully to achieve the same thing by political means.

When historians have come to write about the leadership of the Chartist movement, emotion has usually been as much in evidence as reason. The claim that the movement failed because it was badly led has often sounded less like a calm statement of fact than an indictment in a court of law. There has been a very obvious, if subconscious, feeling that men who were rogues or fools or both ruined a good cause, and that posterity, through the pen, should punish them. A long string of condemnatory verdicts has been handed down: they have been called 'noisy braggards, whose only object is to put money into their purses', and the proceedings of the first Convention have been described as 'the cowardly shufflings of irresolute babblers'. If in general they have been criticised, then, in particular, Feargus O'Connor has been crucified. Gammage, revealing the Victorian obsession with the shape of one's head, surmised that a phrenologist would have pronounced O'Connor strong on perception but weak on reflection, which is mild indeed compared with the character assassination indulged in by Hovell, who saw him as 'the blustering, egotistical, blarneying, managing, but intellectually and morally very unreliable Irishman, who probably had never done an honest day's work in his life'. To him it appeared that 'O'Connor had been using his wealth . . . to buy up a following in the Convention (of 1839)' and that 'he was perhaps the only leading Chartist who was devoid alike of idealism and statesmanship'. Even Gaitskell, who was not over fond of trafficking in abuse, could tartly state that O'Connor 'cared little for education nor morals, having neither in great measure himself'. Of the early leaders, only Lovett has been spared judgements that contain scarcely concealed hostility. Both G. D. H. Cole and Hovell write about him with considerable sympathy. To Cole, although he was 'entirely without the gifts of leadership', he was 'courageous, patient, industrious, rational and devoted'. To Hovell he displayed 'austere morality, unswerving honesty and courage', and his stand against police action in the Bull Ring Riot of 4 July 1839 accomplished more 'than all those who sneered at his moral philosophy and brandished their arms when the enemy was absent'; it was the action of a hero.

Once the anger has been stripped from the historians' judgements, there remains a considerable amount of justifiable criticism. It is clear that for much of the time the leaders failed to lead. In 1839, once it appeared almost certain that the petition would be rejected, decisions had to be taken on the scope and timing of 'ulterior measures'. The Convention had been elected to do just this, but on two vital occasions it suspended its meetings so that delegates could return to their localities in order to gauge the temper of their constituents. Critics see this as an abandonment of the functions of leadership and an attempt to escape the responsibility for taking decisions. Even when the opinions of the rank and file had been discovered, the leaders were particularly hesitant in deducing a plan from them. Place believed that their actions were to be explained by their fear of arrest and prison. Similar charges of cowardice have been levelled at the physical force leaders, who, it is said, led their followers to the brink of the insurrectionary chasm and there left them to topple over if they would. Although there is no foundation for the nineteenth century theory that O'Connor organised an uprising in 1839, of which the Newport Rising was a false start, and then fled to Ireland so as not to be implicated, the general claim that he encouraged his followers to violent action without ever intending to join them seems just. Lovett's reasons for failing to lead have nothing to do with lack of courage. As a firm and doctrinaire believer in democracy, he disliked all forms of leadership, which, he felt, deprived the led of the ability to decide for themselves. He therefore refused to become a leader and was hostile to all those who did not follow his example. A lack of guidance from the top meant that the considerable support engendered by the movement was inefficiently utilised. Chartism here, as in so many respects, contrasts sharply with the Anti-Corn Law League.

The leaders, of course, did not always shirk their duties, and would not have long held their positions, resting as they did on public opinion, if they had. But this has not shielded them from attack, for when they have not been criticised for failing to lead, they have been denounced for leading in the wrong direction. It is with sadness that most historians have recorded the passing of control from the London and Birmingham groups to the North and its leaders, for it was here, it is alleged, that Chartism went off the rails, never to return. From being an intellectual and moderate movement, it became emotional and extreme. But worst of all it adopted the slogan 'peacefully if we may, forcibly if we must', and violence, with all its resulting tragedies, was let in. O'Connor of course has had to bear the brunt of the attack, for it was he who dominated affairs for so long, stamping his personality and ideas deeply into Chartism's history. It was he who made the idea of force respectable among the underprivileged, who wished to fight the tide of industrialisation instead of harnessing it in the interests of the workers, and who led the movement up a blind alley with his futile land scheme. Thus in both aims and methods Chartism was misdirected by those who should have guided it to victory. As it was, an attempt was made to reverse the irreversible in such a way that the most powerful sympathisers were alienated and resources squandered.

Most people who force their way to the top in public life have personal ambition to drive and sustain them. Few indeed are those who find in a good cause alone the incentive necessary to make them struggle on when the situation appears hopeless.

And so historians, over and over again, find themselves attempting to assess the relative importance of selfish and altruistic motives in men's careers. Chartist leaders have on the whole not come out well from this balancing process, and O'Connor, especially, has been accused of being too concerned with his own position. Although it cannot now be seriously held that he aimed to benefit financially from his association with the movement, it is clear that he wished to receive an adoration and acclaim that he increasingly felt were due to him alone. The sychophantic utterances which he encouraged and the expansive self-praise in which he indulged are distasteful to those brought up to be restrained, although it does not follow that they did real harm. Some have suggested that his feuds with other leaders were conducted in order to remove possible rivals and thus safeguard his public position, but the evidence could equally point to a man who wished to safeguard the unity of the movement by eliminating all irrelevant offshoots. That he was particularly vindictive in doing so, and that, as was written at the time, he saw himself as 'a sort of saviour of the working class' (thus regarding all who disagreed with him as unquestionably wrong if not wicked) certainly harmed the cause but does not prove that he had anything but the good of Chartism at heart. He undoubtedly aimed at building up his own prestige, but this was largely done parallel with, rather than in opposition to, his effort to secure the adoption of the Charter.

Chartism was not blessed with good leaders. Their characters often showed serious flaws, their mental abilities (and in O'Connor's case mental stability) were generally open to question, and their previous experience rarely fitted them for the task. They failed to gain the maximum possible support, they lost much support once it had been enlisted, and they misused much of the support that remained. Yet it is possible that Dr. Kitson Clark was right to state that 'however well led or however ill led, the Chartist agitation was without question doomed to failure', for it can be argued that Chartism failed more because of the strength of its opponents than because of the weaknesses of its supporters, leaders and led alike.

The revolutions of 1830 and 1848 in France were only possible because the rulers' will to resist was negligible. Even the First Reform Act and the Repeal of the Corn Laws owed much to the willingness of one portion of the ruling class to accept change rather than risk widespread disturbances. Chartism failed because there was an almost unanimous determination on the part of the owners of property to go to all necessary lengths to defeat what they viewed as an attempt to destroy the existing constitution. That their determination was the result not only of self-interest, but also of a desire both to protect the best interests of the country and to do what was right, made it all the more formidable, for while fear tends to alter ideas of self-interest, it normally strengthens a moral stand. Thus petitions, however widely and genuinely signed, and threats of violence, however spine-chilling, were equally doomed to dismissal by those in power.

Not only had the government the will to resist; it also had the power. By continental standards the British army was very small, and by any standards it was very scattered, but it was still an enormous obstacle to any attempt to overthrow the existing regime, for contrary to the claims of violent leaders who wished to reassure their followers, it was well-disciplined and loyal. Chartists armed with an assortment of makeshift weapons—pikes manufactured out of old files and broomsticks, kitchen knives, broken glass bottles, aqua fortis and old fowling-pieces—could not prevail against even a few thousand well-equipped regulars, even if these were not the force they had been at Waterloo. Without the hope of numerous defections from the ranks of the army, the revolutionaries' only chance was that the troops would be badly led. The appointment of Sir Charles Napier to the command of the Northern District in April 1839, just at the time when advocates of violence were becoming very influential in the manufacturing areas, removed that possibility, for he was a man of courage, experience and sound common sense, as his journal, the main source of our knowledge, amply proves. Realising that if his 6000 troops were distributed throughout the region in small detachments, living in ones and twos in private houses, they would be open to interference and incapable of concerted action, he insisted that they should be gathered together in five large towns and there provided with barracks. He planned to move them to trouble spots, by rail if possible, whenever necessary, and by using large contingents to subdue, through fear, nascent rebellions. Not only did he take steps to ensure that his forces could be used with maximum effect, but he also did his best to discourage Chartist leaders from initiating uprisings. On one famed occasion in Manchester he treated local leaders to an artillery display in the hope that they would understand what effect his eighteen guns could have on a large body of men at close quarters, and in subsequent letters he pointed out to them how easy it would be to massacre a Chartist army as it split up and roamed the country in an unavoidable search for food.

Had the government had no other defence than a few thousand troops, even Napier's cool confidence would have been insufficient to maintain effective law and order. Behind the military, however, there was a multitude of property-owners who were prepared to come to the defence of the society they valued. In 1839 Russell, the Home Secretary, was overwhelmed by demands for arms from local defence forces, and in London in 1848 170,000 special constables, including a large number of domestic servants and the future Napoleon III, were enrolled to prevent whatever disturbances might be planned to coincide with the presentation of the monster petition. Such preparations must have done much to destroy the hopes of those who depended on a short, swift outburst of violence to topple the regime.

In the end one must decide whether the strengths of the government or the weaknesses of the movement constitute the prime cause of Chartism's failure. Professor Briggs, Dr. Kitson Clark and G. D. H. Cole all suggest that the failure of Chartism was inevitable, and it would seem that by this they mean that whatever the Chartists had done, they would have been defeated. By thinking in terms of inevitability (which is always a dangerous thing to do in history), they have chosen to stress those factors that lay beyond the control of the agitators and their followers. But if, in fact, Chartism was a 'repository of lost causes' the story loses much of its drama and pathos, and that would be sad. The optimist believes that all things are possible and, in the best schoolboy tradition, that the game is not lost until the final whistle. Since David slew Goliath lesser men have overcome greater giants and the 'impossible' has been achieved on many occasions. The pig setting out to fly inevitably fails because it attempts to defy the laws of nature; but there was no law of nature which prevented the Charter from becoming law in the 1830s or 1840s. The Chartists set themselves a most difficult task; perhaps they failed chiefly because they were unequal to it.

Chapter II

The Anti-Corn Law League

1 **The problem** In the industrial Midlands and North a new middle class, making its money from the rapidly expanding textile and metallurgical industries, had grown up during the half-century preceding 1830. The members of this class were usually of humble origins, starting their business lives with little capital, and owing their riches to a blend of hard work, honesty, daring, common sense and luck. They were self-made men—*nouveaux-riches*. Before 1830 most of them had been so busy making money that they had had little time for politics.

By 1835 this was changing. The agitation for parliamentary reform between 1830 and 1832 had been joined, at least to the extent of signing petitions or buying pro-reform newspapers, by the majority of the new middle class. Many reverted, once the Reform Act was passed in June 1832, to their former attitudes, 'glorying', in Cobden's words, 'in being the toadies of a clodpole aristocracy, only less enlightened than themselves'. A new crisis was required to make them once again active in public life. The few who had campaigned for reform before 1830, however, were joined by fresh recruits, made politically aware by the events of the Reform Bill crisis. These men were an interesting mixture. There were plenty of young men, their names and fortunes yet to be made, possessed of an idealism that made them wish to change the world; and there were those who had 'arrived' and, success in business already achieved, now had the time and money to accept a new challenge.

To the young men especially, general concepts such as justice were often all-important. Many had imbibed popular versions of the ideas of the political economists and philosophical radicals—Adam Smith, Malthus, Ricardo and Bentham. Along with Bentham, they felt that 'the greatest happiness of the greatest number' was the ideal constantly to be kept in view. They saw an imperfect world around them and blamed it on those who held the reins of power. If only they, who truly understood what was needed, had a real say in the running of the country, they felt, the situation would rapidly improve. Instead of the interests of the few predominating, laws would be passed to further the interests of the many.

The older men tended to view things more personally. Experience, with its lessons of compromise, had ground down their dogmatism and often their selflessness. They had succeeded in life and expected to be treated as men of importance. Yet to be local worthies was not enough. They felt that their contribution to the prosperity of the country had earned them a place at the top of the social scale. 'Industry now stood side by side with hereditary opulence; the owner of ten thousand spindles confronted the lord of ten thousand acres . . . Now the time had arrived when the shadow of an injustice between such rivals could no longer be endured.' It was just this social and political equality with the landed class that they were denied. Wherever the landlord and the industrialist met, the latter was made to feel inferior. In personal contact he was made aware of his outlandish accent, his inability to follow the minutiae of an etiquette with which he had only a nodding acquaintance, his clumsiness in handling the subjects of small talk around which most conversations in society revolved, and his ignorance of the classics, which had a place in most polite conversation. In Parliament in the 1830s he was regarded as an outsider. He was tainted because of the source of his wealth, the 'dark satanic mills' which were believed to be the major feature of such towns as Manchester. Such treatment was the more resented because the values held by the landed aristocracy seemed to be so false. It was easy for the rich industrialist in his hurt pride to claim that the landlords stood for idleness, pettiness, and moral laxity, and to argue that by 'thrusting aside the nobles by force of vigorous intellectual ascendancy, the wealthy middle class should place themselves at the head of a national life with new types and wiser ideals'.

Thus a portion of the middle class was not satisfied with the changes brought about by the Reform Act of 1832 from the moment of its becoming law. They disliked the fact that equality had been denied to industry, for on a basis of population the agricultural South was still three times as well represented as the industrial North. This meant that real power was still in the hands of the landed class and that the interests of Manchester, Leeds and Birmingham could still be ignored.

The majority, however, believed that the reformed system would be totally satisfactory. The right to return Members of Parliament had been given to the large towns of the Midlands and North, and these new representatives would be able to voice their opinions at Westminster. The vote had been given to the respectable middle-class inhabitants of the towns, and thus the M.P.s would be true representatives of the merchants and manufacturers. It was only when the reformed Parliament failed to maintain the mild prosperity of the mid-thirties that dissatisfaction with the new system became widespread. Then, because their economic position was threatened by a general falling off in trade, the manufacturers, who were normally absorbed in their businesses, were prepared to listen to those who argued that only a fresh agitation would put things right.

2 **The ideal solution** In the years immediately after 1832 those of the industrial middle class who continued to agitate did so very much as individuals or members of small groups. This is not surprising, as their experience of life had taught them to rely mainly on themselves, to form their ideas independently and to beware of following others. Thus Parliament and the provinces witnessed a rash of minor movements, each aiming at a different objective, and each unaware that only the united forces of radicalism could hope to achieve anything

against a landlord-dominated system. So, while some devoted their time to the cause of state primary education, others campaigned for the secret ballot, currency reform, an extension of the franchise, or the repeal of the Corn Laws. It is perhaps needless to say that in this period no changes in the laws relating to these subjects were made.

On 24 September 1838 seven men met in a small room in Manchester and decided to set up a Manchester Anti-Corn Law Association, open to all who would pay the annual subscription of five shillings. During the first week fifty, and during the second week one hundred, local capitalists were persuaded to join. In the following January a dinner was held in Manchester for the representatives of other local Anti-Corn Law Associations, and on 20 March delegates meeting in London set up the National Anti-Corn Law League.

Some members of the League in their writings would have us believe that from the early days of the agitation the majority of middle-class Radicals, agreeing with Cobden that 'the English people cannot be made to take up more than one question at a time with enthusiasm', gave up their separate campaigns to join with the League, which refused to discuss or work for anything besides the repeal of the Corn Laws. It is certainly true that massive support was gained from the towns of South Lancashire and North Staffordshire, and that many from the Midlands and West Riding of Yorkshire also joined in, but considerable numbers of the middle class, especially in Birmingham and Leeds, preferred to inaugurate movements aiming at a further extension of the franchise. It is unrealistic to see the Anti-Corn Law agitation as monopolising urban middle-class zeal in the years after 1838.

Yet the fact remains that for large numbers Repeal became a panacea. They believed that once corn could be imported freely at all times, instead of being subject to a large duty even when prices on the home market were unseasonably high, their many and varied hopes would be fulfilled. How was this to be? How was Repeal to bring about a complete change in the social and political structure and the end of periodic economic slumps?

There is no shortage of evidence on what the Leaguers thought the effects of Repeal would be. Speeches made in Parliament and quoted in Hansard, speeches made at meetings and paraphrased or, thanks to the invention towards the end of the crusade of a workable system of shorthand, quoted verbatim in sympathetic newspapers; tracts and pamphlets issued by the League; and the many surviving letters of supporters all contain, over and over again, the arguments used to convince the uncommitted that the Corn Laws must go.

One argument much used at first to win over the cotton cloth manufacturers of Lancashire, but then dropped as bad for the popular image of the League, was well summed up by the posters with which Chartists plastered the walls of the Manchester Town Hall one night when an Anti-Corn Law meeting was due to take place there. 'Why do these liberal manufacturers bawl so lustily for the repeal of the Corn Laws? Because, with the reduced price of corn, they will be enabled to reduce the wages of the working men, in order that they may compete with foreigners who live upon potatoes.' To the manufacturer who was finding it hard to sell his products the prospect of lower wages was highly attractive. He could either reap his reward immediately in increased profits, or by lowering prices increase his competitive position in foreign markets. It is no wonder that one manufacturer wrote to a friend saying that if the Corn Laws were repealed he would make ten times his £100 contribution to the League in higher profits.

At the free trade meeting which directly stimulated the foundation of the Manchester Association in 1838, Dr. Bowring the visiting speaker described conversations which he had recently had on the Continent. He reported the farmers of Normandy and Brittany as having said, 'Admit our corn and then we'll see whether anybody can prevent the importation of your manufactures into France. We are millions willing to clothe ourselves in the garments you send us, and you have millions of hungry mouths to take our corn.' Countless times variations on this theme were propounded from Anti-Corn Law platforms, until they constituted the major economic argument in favour of Repeal. Readers of League literature could hardly resist the belief that there were millions in Europe and America waiting to buy Lancashire's cloth, but unable to do so because the lack of a market for their surplus grain left them without hard cash. If only foreign corn could enter Britain duty-free, European and American farmers would be put in possession of large amounts of money which they would naturally spend on the manufactured goods of Britain. Thus the market for cotton and woollen cloth, metal goods and pottery would be greatly extended and the workshops and factories would be at full production for evermore. The manufacturer would be gaining the same profit per item as before, but as more would be sold his total profit would be considerably increased.

This argument came to stand in opposition to the original wage reduction theory, for it allowed League spokesmen to declare that far from wages being reduced they would actually be increased. When labour was greatly in demand, it was stated, wages rose, and when there was little demand they fell. In the post-repeal situation of almost unlimited markets, labour would be in short supply and consequently wages would be raised in order to attract workers.

Although the negatively harmful economic effect of the Corn Laws, in stopping the exploitation of potential markets, was most frequently stressed, speakers often dwelt on the positively harmful side as well. They claimed that existing sales were endangered because European landowners, seeing little point in investing their capital in an agricultural industry which was denied Britain as an outlet, turned their attention to manufacturing instead. Thus industrialisation in France, the Low Countries, Germany, and, it was even claimed, Hungary, was being encouraged by the British Corn Laws. When this was coupled with the fact that foreign governments, allegedly infuriated at the refusal of this country to accept their agricultural products freely, were maintaining, or even imposing, high tariff walls against British manufacturers, thus allowing their own nascent industries to flourish, the Lancashire mill-owner was quite prepared to believe that if things remained unchanged he would soon be able to sell nothing abroad. Not only would the end of the Corn Laws bring added prosperity—the failure to repeal them would actually lead to ruin.

Although a large proportion of the new middle class was most concerned about the economy, there were many who saw the repeal of the Corn Laws as a way of changing the social and political balance of the country. A *Times* leader of November 1843 admitted that its readers would say of the League that 'its object is not to open the ports, to facilitate commerce, to enrich England, but to ruin our aristocracy, whom Leaguers envy and detest'. Much of the verbally violent opposition to the Anti-Corn Law movement sprang from the belief of many landowners that the real object was to ruin them socially and politically. They had good reason to think as they did. A full-time agent of the League wrote in 1840 that 'Lord Stanley's party is better to be humbled by repeal of the Corn Laws than any other way'. And he was not untypical of the movement's less idealistic members. For them the most desirable result of Repeal would be the ruin of British agriculture and of those who depended on it for their unearned wealth. Once the Dukes and Marquises were denied their huge rentals they would be unable to play their accustomed social and political roles. At last dominance would pass to the people who really created the country's wealth. At its most parochial, expressed by Cobden in an uncharacteristically ungenerous moment, this philosophy longed for the day when 'Liverpool and Manchester will more and more assume their proper rank as commercial capitals and London must content itself with a gambling trade in the bills drawn by those places'. Not even the mercantile class of the metropolis was to be spared.

In a court of law it is often very difficult to establish the real motives of those on trial. For the historian, who cannot recall his witnesses from the grave for questioning and who must rely on the fragments that have somehow survived, the problem of deciding motivation is even more perplexing, and is increased by the fact that evidence was often intended to be used by posterity. Public figures knew that their letters and speeches would be pounced upon by historians in years to come, and so adapted what they wrote and said to fit in with what they hoped would be the verdict of the future. When studying the events of more than a century ago, it is frequently impossible to disentangle the web of pretended and real beliefs. When one asks, 'Were the Leaguers selfishly seeking what was of advantage to themselves, or hoping to benefit mankind, Britain, and other groups within the community?' one must not expect a clear-cut answer.

The enemies of the League—the landlords, the Chartists and those whose fear of social revolution made them detest any popular agitation—found the question very easy to answer. To them the movement was led and supported by brash and uneducated mill-owners who wished to ruin agriculture in order to improve their own economic position. That they cared only for themselves was proved by the terrible conditions in which they forced their workers to live and labour. It was felt that they should put their own house in order before telling others that in passing the Corn Laws they had committed 'a crime of the deepest dye against the rights of industry and against the well-being of the British people'. Even Archibald Prentice, a founder member of the Manchester Association, and second most regular attender of its meetings through the years, had to admit in his *History of the Anti-Corn Law League*, published in 1853, that most supporters felt that they had something to gain from Repeal. But, he hastened to intone, 'Happy it is when the interest of a class is the interest of the whole community'. Many other defenders echoed him by arguing that there is nothing wrong in helping yourself when you help others at the same time—enlightened self-interest.

There can be no doubt that many League supporters felt that they were doing more than trying to line their own pockets. For many it was a struggle to obtain justice from the landowners, who taxed the bread of the poor in order to enrich themselves, or a fight to improve the lot of the working man by making his bread cheaper and ensuring him regular and well-paid employment. That many employers felt strongly about the hardships endured by the urban unemployed is dramatically proved by the scene in the reception room of the Chancellor of the Exchequer as, in March 1840, one of a large deputation of Leaguers described the sufferings of an industrious Manchester family. Tears rolled down the cheeks of Joseph Sturge, one of the listening visitors, and few of the deputation could boast a tearless eye. Is it surprising that 'the ministers looked with perfect astonishment at a scene so unusual to statesmen and courtiers'?

Some of the leaders of the movement hoped that Repeal would be the first step 'along a path which was to lead to international interdependence and lasting peace'. The belief was that once the nations of the world were freely trading one with another, war would become too disruptive to be countenanced. Peace would be further assured by the new social and political systems which would rapidly evolve in Britain after Repeal. The old feudal landowning class, whose main *raison d'être* had been war, would be replaced by the more godly commercial classes, whose interests would be furthered by peace. Thus the destruction of aristocratic rule would be a moral rather than a selfish act.

It is clear that the motives of most of the Leaguers were far from the extremes of pure selfishness and unmixed benevolence. To generalise further about a group of such mixed character and status, most of whom are no more than names on a subscription list, would be unwise. People are seldom all bad or all good, and those who claim to be either are usually deceiving themselves.

3 Ways and means   There are two ways of achieving success open to people who wish to obtain an alteration in the law of the land. They may persuade the legislature to take the appropriate action, or they may overthrow the regime and replace it with one that will fulfil their desires. In the half-century before 1835 the people of France, or more especially Paris, had frequently chosen the latter mode, in contrast with the British, who had been blessed with a ruling class which knew how to bend with the wind. Considerable change had come peacefully to this country in the years since 1820, and we now know that the trend was to be continued. For the people of England who had just lived through the Reform Bill crisis of 1831-2 there was no such certainty. They were only too aware, as was a newspaper editor in 1838, that 'there needs but a spark to ignite the mass of smouldering discontent'.

The leaders of the Anti-Corn Law League at no time suggested that they should foment a revolution or engineer a *coup d'état*. The nearest they came to this type of action was in 1842, when at least some members of the League's Council were in favour of adding to the prevailing unrest in the hope of producing a situation in which the government must yield or risk a complete breakdown of law and order. Although the claims of a hostile press that the League was directly responsible for the Plug Plot Riots are almost certainly unfounded, there is strong evidence to suggest that John Bright, the textile manufacturer from Rochdale whose powers of oratory made him the League's most effective public speaker, seriously advocated a concerted lock-out by employers in the industrial areas so that the despair bred of already extensive unemployment would be heightened. Others favoured a run on the banks and a refusal to pay all taxes in order to produce a financial crisis. In both cases the aim was to make the government give way, and not to overthrow the existing system by force.

Thus even the most radical members of the League accepted that persuasion must be their method. Such was the confidence of the Repealers that their case was based on 'the high and impregnable foundations of immutable truth and justice' that most believed nothing else would be necessary. Yet even when it had been agreed that conversion by the force of logical argument was the technique to be employed the targets for their propaganda still had to be selected.

New political movements often appear to change considerably during their early days as initial enthusiasms are tempered by contact with reality, and pitfalls are found in the seemingly broad and straight road to success. So it was with the Manchester Anti-Corn Law Association during its first few months of existence in late 1838 and early 1839. At the outset the organisers seem to have been so overwhelmed by the self-evident truth of their arguments that they acted as if the trumpet only needed to sound for the tariff walls to fall. They advocated a campaign of lectures in all areas, presuming that the conversion of large numbers of people would secure Repeal. By January 1839 a greater degree of practicality had become evident, for it was decided that deputations from each of the important manufacturing areas should be organised, and should meet in London. Permission would be sought to present the arguments against the Corn Laws to the House of Commons, and it was presumed that M.P.s, seeing the light for the first time, would hasten to introduce the necessary legislation. Here was a plan that, in theory at least, could end in victory.

On 19 February a motion in the Commons that the evidence of the assembled Repealers should be heard was defeated by 361 votes to 172. Although one or two of the less naive members of the deputation were not surprised, the majority could hardly believe that such a thing had happened. Much woolly-headed optimism was dispelled as it became clear in that moment that truth and justice do not always triumph in politics. Frustrated, and with pride hurt, but resolve unshaken, the northerners retreated to their homeland in order to devise new tactics. 'The delegates had offered to instruct the House; the House had refused to be instructed. The House must be instructed; and the way now contemplated was the grandest and most unexceptionable and effectual—it was to be by instructing the nation.' A month later the Anti-Corn Law League was founded, in theory a combination of equal local associations but in practice the Manchester Association writ large, and for five years the instruction of the nation was to be its chief though unsolicited mission.

Most historians of the nineteenth century, following the lead given by Prentice, portrayed the story of the League as an uninterrupted march to inevitable triumph. Knowing what the result was to be and having little but Prentice and the pro-League press to use as evidence, they would have found it difficult to come to any other conclusion. Prentice saw the Leaguers, himself included, as a band of knights attacking the citadel of Monster Monopoly, and he was unprepared to spoil the image by admitting that doubts ever assailed the trusty warriors. Perhaps, as he sat and dreamed of the glorious days now past, he even forgot that such things had existed, but doubts there had been. It was not that the Leaguers ever lost faith in the righteousness of their cause, but that they wondered whether their methods could ever bring success.

To have carried the campaign from Parliament to the nation may have seemed brave and splendid, but it is the former and not the latter which makes the laws. The League leaders tried to convince themselves that 'we have a public opinion here that is not uninfluential'. The theory was that Members of Parliament would appreciate the strength of feeling that existed 'out of doors' and would give the people what they wanted. If that did not work, then the electors would, when the Commons were next dissolved, choose men who would listen to the popular voice. As repeated demonstrations of support failed to move any but the 125 or so free trade sympathisers in the Commons, and as the likelihood of an election dominated by the League diminished, most of the prominent League supporters lost heart. An indication of their despair is given by one biographer, who, in his search for John Bright's major contribution to the repeal struggle, overlooked his great powers of oratory and chose instead his work as 'morale-lifter'. He had constantly to insist to his co-workers that there was hope. Despite this they were periodically overwhelmed by the fear that their method was not the 'grandest and most effectual'.

Nevertheless the work went on. At first the greatest effort was made in the industrial areas, where it was presumed that 'natural' support would exist. Success was such that by the early months of 1843 the League was confident enough to mount a twin offensive on the metropolis and on the country-side. By the late summer of the next year Richard Cobden, the country-bred Manchester businessman whose sincerity and industry had secured for him a pre-eminent position in the League, was prepared to claim that the work of instruction had been completed.

Never before had England, or to a lesser extent Scotland, been subjected to such a well-organised and all-pervading propaganda campaign. Every device known to the publicist, and many which until then were not, was called upon to aid the cause. In the days before cinema, radio and television a public meeting could be guaranteed to attract an audience, no matter what the subject. The League took full advantage of this, and from the beginning used the lecture as one of the main vehicles for its message. In 1839 three full-time travelling lecturers were recruited. In the next year the number was increased, and although both the schemes had to be abandoned in mid-summer because money ran out, the idea was held to be good enough for a paid secretary-cum-lecturer to be appointed to each of the twelve districts into which the country was divided when the League was reorganised in 1842. To begin with, the prominent members felt that it would be unseemly for themselves to address meetings outside their own localities. Once this reluctance was overcome in 1840, and especially from late 1841 when Cobden and Bright decided to devote much of their time to this activity, nearly every town of any size in England and Scotland was treated to a visit from one or other of the leaders of the movement. The speakers often showed their belief in the unanswerable nature of their arguments by inviting local spokesmen of the protectionist interest to appear on the same platform with them. At first many did, but as they consistently came off worse, volunteers became increasingly scarce. Many of the early meetings were held in small rooms, often above the bar of a public house, but this did not for long satisfy those who were determined to show the nation that the League was a force to be reckoned with. As no suitably large building existed in Manchester a special Free Trade Hall was erected on the site of the Peterloo Massacre, and in it eight or nine thousand people could assemble, often to hear three or four speakers, each of whom would remain on his feet for more than an hour. For the major London campaign of 1843-4 the Drury Lane Theatre and then Covent Garden were hired, and weekly meetings, attended by large and respectable audiences, were held.

The League recognised in the written word a weapon that could well compete with the spoken word in the struggle to win over the respectable portions of society. Newspapers were especially useful as they would often be regarded as impartial and their support would therefore be more convincing. This was not true of the League's own periodical, which at first appeared fortnightly and then, from September 1843, weekly, and which was mainly aimed at 'keeping a constant correspondence with the local associations', nor of such obviously partisan publications as Prentice's own *Manchester Times*. The nominally independent press was what the League was after. The normal ways of influencing them were much less open than the grants of money which were made to one or two journals. Instead, advertisements, always an important source of income for the low-circulation papers of the time, were placed only with those editors who gave glowing reports in return. Free reports of League meetings were sent to papers in the hope that they would be included, and they often were, as editors with few or no reporters were pleased to be presented with ready-made copy. Most effective of all was the promise to buy large numbers—sometimes as much as a third of the normal circulation—of those issues which had particularly lengthy or favourable reports. These were then distributed by the League where it was thought 'they would do most good'.

Far fewer people were reached by any one newspaper article than by the more popular of the League pamphlets, even if Prentice's claim that the 15,000 copies of the *Anti-Corn Law Circular* were read by 200,000 people is less exaggerated than it seems. The pamphlets were composed of from four to sixteen pages of small print and were systematically produced from the spring of 1839 onwards. The early issues were sold at cost price to distributors all over the country as well as being circulated by the travelling lecturers. In November 1842 a most ambitious scheme was launched. Every elector was to have delivered to his door, by full- or part-time paid helpers, a packet of pamphlets arguing for Repeal and against protection. This, to all intents and purposes, was accomplished. In 1840 one and a quarter million tracts were produced. At the end of 1843 the League leaders, who gloried in the sheer size of their effort, could announce that in the last year nine million tracts, weighing over 100 tons, had been dispatched from the Manchester headquarters.

While all this thinking big was in progress the details were not being overlooked. For 1/- anybody could buy eighteen sheets of wafers inside a pretty cover. These were small pieces of paper used to stick down letters in the days before gummed envelopes, and each one produced by the League carried a two- or three-line motto which summarised a part of the case for Repeal. For much less one could purchase a sheet of woodcuts which showed in graphic form the hardships caused by the bread monopoly.

Cobden never admitted that the educating of the nation was the best way of destroying the Corn Laws. He agreed that it was useful but he was much more in favour of putting pressure directly on Parliament. It was he who insisted that delegates should assemble in London whenever the Commons discussed the subject, so that nobody would be in any doubt about the feeling of the country. Besides passing their own resolutions, so that they could be fully quoted in the press, those assembled saw any ministers who would receive them. In 1842 none would, so over five hundred delegates marched to Westminster to lobby M.P.s. Refused entry there, they gave three rousing cheers for Repeal that none inside could have failed to hear. But such behaviour, not being that of gentlemen, convinced many landowners that the manufacturers were indeed little better than working men.

Each year, normally towards the end of March, Charles Villiers introduced a motion into the Commons advocating the repeal of the Corn Laws. His efforts antedated the foundation of the League and he never fully fitted into the movement. None the less, in deference to him, its leaders made his motion their parliamentary highlight of the year. The debate normally continued over four or five nights before the House divided and the motion was decisively defeated. Cobden, elected M.P. for Stockport in 1841, saw these discussions as more than just extra publicity. Although he realised that there was no hope of winning over a majority of M.P.s, he did feel that there was a possibility of converting members of the government, especially Peel. This was the main objective of his parliamentary campaign, for he knew that a ministerially sponsored Bill would probably pass into law.

Cobden also hoped to be able to affect the composition of Parliament. To him, the usefulness of the nation-wide propaganda campaign was that it prepared electors to support free trade candidates. The more cautious of the League's leaders did not wish the movement to become directly political. Although Cobden agreed with them that to set up a separate party would be to risk losing the support of those who put their liberalism or conservatism before the cause of Repeal, he argued that every effort should be made to secure the return of as many sympathetic candidates as possible. A motion to this effect was passed by delegates in March 1840, but it was not a popular decision. The failure of the League to make a real impact on the 1841 election was a fairer reflection of its policy at this stage than was the backing of a free trade candidate in the Walsall by-election of December 1840. It was not until September 1843 that Cobden's ideas were really accepted. Then it was decided that a League-sponsored candidate would be put forward whenever a borough seat fell vacant, and although this task proved too enormous to carry out fully, great efforts were made.

In July 1844 a new technique was adopted. In about seventy constituencies efforts were made to have hostile voters struck off the electoral roll as unqualified, and to have the names of free traders added. Every type of chicanery was resorted to, and in South Lancashire at least, with success. Here 878 protectionists lost the right to vote and 2821 free traders gained it. This was enough to make the seats safe for supporters of the League. At the same time a campaign to create, rather than merely register, electors was commenced. Repealers were urged to buy sufficient property to give themselves the vote by one of the many qualifications that existed. To make things easier a special form was printed. The man wishing to procure a vote merely had to fill it in and send off the required amount of money—usually £50–70—to the League, which would arrange the purchase of suitable property for him.

To carry on its varied activities the League required money. Lack of it had curtailed the activities of 1839 and 1840, but from then on the finances were placed on a sounder footing. A £50,000 fund was started in October 1842, followed the next year by one for £100,000, and in December 1845 by one for £250,000. The first two were duly raised and spent, and only the repeal of the Corn Laws in 1846 prevented the achievement of the third target. Throughout the life of the League donations from supporters made up the bulk of its income. Experience and the need for ever-increasing sums of money led to the development of more sophisticated methods of eliciting these contributions. To begin with subscriptions gained from personal approaches were eked out by collections made at meetings. The establishment of a £50 donation as the qualification for membership of the League's Council gave an incentive to more generous attitudes, as did the opening of the three large-scale funds. In operating these the League could have learnt little from modern money-raising experts. The quarter-million pound appeal was announced at a mass meeting in the Free Trade Hall, and after the audience had been brought to a highly emotional state by the speakers, the chairman requested that they should write their promised contributions on their cards and pass them to the front. For one-and-a-half-hours during mounting excitement names and amounts were read from the platform. By the end more than £60,000 had been pledged, much of it no doubt by those who wondered later why they had allowed themselves to be so carried away. Most remarkable of all the League's fund-raising activities were the two Bazaars. The first, at the Theatre Royal, Manchester, in early 1842, pales when compared with the one held at Covent Garden in May 1845. Both were national efforts, each locality stocking a stall with a selection of its most attractive products, but only the second Bazaar could boast such a variety of choice items that one historian could compare it with the Great Exhibition of six years later. The result was the raising of £25,000 for League funds, as opposed to a third of that amount in 1842. Three guineas had even been given for a lock of Sir Walter Scott's hair.

4 Success or failure? It is not surprising that the Repealers considered the repeal of the Corn Laws (see below pp. 84-90) to be very much their triumph, as they had worked for eight years to achieve it, or that writers such as Prentice took it for granted that the change in the law was directly attributable to the efforts of the Manchester men, when Peel, speaking of Repeal in his resignation speech, could say, 'Sir, the name which ought to be, and will be, associated with the success of these measures . . . is the name of Richard Cobden. Without scruple, Sir, I attribute the success of these measures to him.' Yet it is not obvious that the members of the Anti-Corn Law League deserve the credit, for it was Peel who in 1846 introduced the Bill, fought it through Parliament, and lost office because of it. At the time, the League's supporters were in a minority in the Commons and not one was a member of the government. To go to the other extreme, however, and suggest that the League was in no way responsible would clearly be silly. Many historians have settled on the League's conversion of Peel as its major success. It is difficult, however, to decide just what caused the Prime Minister to lose faith in the Corn Laws. It is traditional to stress the effect of Cobden's speeches during debate in Parliament, and especially that of 13 March 1845, during which Peel, who was expected to reply, dramatically crumpled up his notes, and turning to Sidney Herbert, said, 'You must answer this, for I cannot.' It seems likely, though, that this speech made Peel aware that his mind had changed rather than changed it for him. Certainly Prentice is much too willing to see Peel as a tormented soul whose conscience was troubled by the League until he could resist no longer. He describes an occasion in 1842 when five hundred Anti-Corn Law marchers were passed by the Prime Minister, who was so affected that 'he leaned back in his carriage, grave and pale'. No doubt the marchers believed they had such an impact, but it must have been wishful thinking. On the other hand Miss Ramsay probably gave the League too little credit when she wrote that Peel's conversion 'was partly due to the convincing eloquence of Cobden and Bright, but more to his own observation of facts'. She was right to stress that Peel was the type of man to think things out for himself, rather than to be converted by force of emotion, but she failed to mention that the facts which Peel observed were those that were brought to his notice by Anti-Corn Law publicists, for unlike his father and grandfather, he had no experience of the life lived by those outside his own class. In Peel's case it seems that the League's policy of presenting people with the facts paid off.

The researches of recent years have established that the numbers persuaded by the League to oppose the Corn Laws were not as great as had previously been thought. The campaign to win over tenant farmers and agricultural labourers, in particular, has been shown to have been far less successful than claimed. This forces one to modify the old view that the country was by 1846 generally in favour of Repeal, but it does not alter the fact that by making people believe that the Corn Laws were unpopular, the League made their abolition a practical proposition. If it had not been for the propaganda work of the free traders, Russell would not have declared in favour of Repeal in November 1845 in an effort to attract support, and the Whigs would not have been morally obliged to ensure the passage of the Corn Bill through the Commons by supporting it. Peel would not have been so keen to go against his party in order to do what he felt to be right, if he had not been able to argue that in opposing the majority of Conservatives he was pleasing a majority in the country, and the Lords would have been less willing to follow the advice of Wellington and pass the Bill if they had not been convinced of the strength of popular feelings. Thus the League deserves credit not only for its part in converting Peel but also for creating an atmosphere in which Repeal could be passed.

To the League the repeal of the Corn Laws was success, but the historian must ask whether the reform achieved all that was expected of it. Those who hoped for the ruin of agriculture and of the landlord class which depended on it were disappointed, as were those who had predicted a sudden lowering of bread prices, for there existed no large-scale supply of cheap foreign grain which could be imported to undercut the home producer. Thus the quinquennial average price of wheat per quarter was: 54/9 in 1841-6, 51/10 in 1846-50, and 56/- in 1851-5. This has led some commentators to conclude that the League had been fighting a phantom and that Repeal had no real effect until low rail and steamer charges allowed cheap American corn to be imported in the late 1870s. Such an opinion contrasts sharply with that of some nineteenth-century historians who unquestioningly accepted that the mid-century period of prosperity was a direct result of Peel's action in 1846. That there is evidence to support both views suggests that the truth lies somewhere in between, but as yet our understanding of the effect of the Corn Laws and of their removal on international trade is so limited that no certain answer can be given to the wider questions. In a more limited way, however, it is possible to note that wheat prices would, in all probability, have risen considerably during the 1850s and 1860s had the Corn Laws remained, in part because of world-wide inflationary pressures, but more especially because a rapidly increasing population had by 1850 made it necessary to import one quarter of the country's grain requirements even in good years. In this case prices must have risen to cover the duty being paid on such a sizeable proportion of the wheat supply. Thus, even if it should be proved that the Corn Laws were not adversely affecting the economy in the 1840s, there remains the League's achievement of having prevented them from doing so in the decades that followed.

Chapter III

Peel and the Conservative Party

1 The man Sir Robert Peel (1788-1850) appeared to come from the upper class. He grew up on the family's estate of Drayton, near Tamworth, which his father, an M.P. from 1790 and a baronet from 1800, had bought soon after his son's birth. When old enough he was sent to Harrow and later became a gentleman commoner at Christ Church, Oxford. As a twenty-first birthday present his father provided him with a seat in Parliament. Yet the Peels were essentially middle-class. Peel's grandfather, having begun life as a yeoman farmer, became a wealthy manufacturer and printer of cotton cloth in Blackburn, and his father made an even larger fortune in the same trade at Bury before establishing himself as a country squire in the Midlands. A broad Lancashire accent survived the transition from manufacturer to landed gentleman, and traces of it remained in the son throughout his life. The outlook and standards of the family were those of the business classes, and Peel was taught as a boy to look upon life as a struggle for personal advancement in which those who worked hardest and with honesty achieved most. He was left in no doubt that his duty was to work his way to the top.

Peel was an ideal son, for he attempted at all times to live up to his father's expectations. He worked extremely hard, was scrupulously honest, and accepted all sound advice that was offered him. As a result he made good use of his ample intelligence to become the first person under the new Oxford regulations to obtain a double first. His abilities, however, had their limitations, for although he possessed a ready under-standing, a remarkable memory and an instinctive sense of leadership, he lacked the imagination which is an essential aspect of genius. Thus present reality rather than a dream of the future tended to be all-important to him. Guizot, who saw him as a 'man of essentially practical mind, consulting facts at every step, just as the mariner consults the face of heaven', considered this to be praiseworthy, but Dr. Kitson Clark has blamed him for being 'content to do his work with a blurred background, pollarded principles and no very ardent or exten-sive desires'. Halévy, in more neutral vein, characterised him as 'an opportunist who took his often energetic decisions with an eye to the wishes of the country and the needs of the moment'. The narrowing of vision produced by his matter-of-fact attitude was increased by the certainty that he was embarked on a successful and valuable career. This led him to become more hot-tempered, self-satisfied, prejudiced and even 'priggish, imperious and overbearing' as the years passed. Some believed that his arrogance was only matched by his ambition.

In part the critics who thought Peel too self-important were misled by his manner, for his unsmiling, almost frigid formality was not totally disdainful. He was by nature shy and lacking in self-confidence, and although he learnt largely to overcome this, he still found it necessary to shelter behind an icy exterior on occasions, for he was easily hurt by the criticisms or hostility of others. Perhaps his was the 'reserve characteristic of those primarily concerned in coming to terms with themselves rather than with the outside world'. Peel, however, was not totally engrossed in his problems and ambitions. He was capable of forming deep and lasting relationships with his wife and family and with colleagues such as Aberdeen, in which he gave freely of his time, energies, ideas and emotions. But it was not only in his private life that he proved to be a kind as well as a good man, for while in office he constantly kept in mind the feelings and well-being of others, even being prepared to insist that convicts, on sailing for Australia, should be provided with two pairs of woollen drawers instead of one!

2 In opposition From April 1835 to September 1841 Peel led the Conservative party in opposition to Lord Melbourne's Whig government. This was not a new experience, for he had been the chief opposition spokesman in the Commons during the four years that had separated the demise of Wellington's ministry from the birth of his own short-lived minority government in December 1834. Nor were the problems he faced entirely novel. In the past many leaders of parties or factions fallen from power had had to design a strategy that would bring them back to high office. Yet for Peel, the task was particularly difficult. No longer was there the mighty Tory party which had held office, almost without interruption, from 1784 to 1830, and which he had loyally supported from 1809. Instead there remained a party which, having lost its more progressive members to the Whigs in 1830, had been reduced to a rump of about one hundred and fifty by the election of December 1832.

Electoral setbacks were proved, however, to be reversible when nearly a hundred extra supporters of Peel were returned in 1835. More worrying were the disunity and mistrust within the Conservative party. These were mainly caused by the personalities of the leaders. The leader in the Lords, who until 1834 had been regarded by most as the head of the party, was the Duke of Wellington. He had proved on the battlefields of Europe that he was straightforward and courageous, but he was not well suited to the game of politics, where flexibility and imagination are sometimes essential attributes. By adopting a stern, but rigid and unwise, opposition to reform in 1830 he had hastened the collapse of his government, and increasingly Tory peers were prepared to accept guidance from other men, such as Lyndhurst, the ex-Lord Chancellor, who lacked none of the wiles of the politician. Thus it was often with great difficulty that reactionary peers were persuaded to toe the official line. To make matters worse, there was very little co-operation between the Conservatives in the Lords and those in the Commons. At times, several months went by without contact between Peel and Wellington, and such correspondence as there was, was often of a most general nature. Certainly there was very little in the way of concerted action. This was partly because Peel did not consider it his duty to guide the party in the Lords, but largely because of the lack of confidence which existed between the leader and his supporters among the peers. Thus the execution of any strategy aimed at the recovery of power was made more difficult. In the Commons Peel was faced by no open challenge to his authority, for even those who disliked him had, sullenly, to admit that there was no-one in the House who could rival his reputation. Instead, there sat behind him many men who doubted his honour, and who supported him only because there was no-one else to follow. They believed that in 1829 he had acted unforgivably over the problem of Catholic Emancipation*, when, after years of declared opposition to the measure, he had remained in office in order to pilot it through the Commons. They rationalised their prejudice against him by deciding that it was, after all, the typical action of an ill-bred fellow. This was not a situation that augured well for the future.

Divisions, however, were created by measures as well as by men. While some had persuaded themselves that all reform was dangerous and wrong, many had come to the conclusion that only by correcting obvious abuses could the sound part of the constitution be saved. Peel passionately, and Wellington reluctantly, were of the latter opinion, and many of the stresses within the party were the result of the leaders' efforts to ensure the passage of the Whig government's more necessary reforms. Although the party's weakness and disunity were disconcerting, it was the impression that the tide of history was running against the Conservatives which caused the greatest consternation. Since 1830 the desire for political change had been the most obvious preoccupation of the country, and instead of being damped down by the Act of 1832, the enthusiasm and influence of reformers had been increased. It was encouraging

* See J. W. Hunt, *Reaction and Reform 1815-1841* in this series

for Conservatives to gain so many seats in the 1835 election, but a surer sign of the times seemed to be the success achieved by the Radical reformers, who doubled their numbers and won nearly every metropolitan seat. Where London led, the rest of the country would surely follow. It was not only Peel's Tory friend Croker who believed that succeeding years would witness a series of ever more extreme Radical governments.

In the years following the passage of the Reform Act, Peel worked to re-fashion the old Tory party into a new Conservative party which would one day bring him to power by winning a general election. He used his position as chief Opposition spokesman in the Commons to voice his rapidly developing ideas, but made no attempt to force all Tories to accept his creed, for he realized that the process of conversion could not be hurried, and was convinced that nothing must be done that would make it impossible for any moderate man to join him in the future. Professor Gash has written that 'Peel's work was meaningless if it did not stand for a widening of the party's social foundations'. He especially stresses Peel's efforts to gain support from moderate middle-class reformers, and it was indeed such people, and their representatives in Parliament, whom the Conservative leader hoped to attract as the years went by. This he could only do by offering them a philosophy which they would find more acceptable than the ideas enshrined in the dangerously vague utterances of the Whig leaders. This he did in the Tamworth Manifesto of 1835, which, although addressed to his constituents, was aimed at the country, and in a series of speeches both inside and outside Parliament.

Peel presumed that the 'sober-minded and well-disposed (but as yet non-Conservative) portion of the community' was as concerned as he was about the increasing lack of public order, and the danger of reforms being passed which would further question the sanctity of private property and the utility of the existing constitution. Therefore he could confidently pronounce that besides accepting the 1832 Reform Act, he stood for strong government, the conservation of all that was sound in the existing system, and the reform of proven abuses, for such a combination of aims could hardly fail to appeal to the majority of the newly enfranchised middle classes. What is surprising is that the Whigs did not think to take up a similar position. It was, after all, little different from their traditional policy. Peel was perhaps on less sure ground when he developed his ideas on retaining the existing framework of the constitution. His plan to defend the prerogative of the Crown, the privileges of the House of Lords and the rights of the Church of England was attacked in 1844 by Disraeli as 'forms and phrases' that had no substance. Although much of the adverse comment which forms Book II Chapter 5 of *Coningsby* is unfair, it is true that Peel liked the theory of kingly and lordly power more than he did the practice. Yet in this he was joined by many who saw the continued political independence of the monarch and the upper House as the symbol of a world that seemed to be fast vanishing, but which they generally admired.

Whenever Lord Melbourne's ministry acted in a responsible manner Peel openly and heartily supported it, although he took care to stress that a Conservative government with a majority would be more in the country's interests. Such action was in part designed to impress high-minded men with the reasonable and non-partisan nature of the Conservative party, but was also aimed at securing the continuance of the present ministry. On many occasions the government was only saved from a defeat in the Commons by the support provided by the Opposition, but it was with difficulty that Peel persuaded many of his followers of the wisdom of his policy. To those who wished to combine with dissident Radicals in order to bring down the government, he explained that such a procedure would lead to the formation of a weak and short-lived Conservative government, to be followed either by an equally weak Radical government, or by a reinstated Melbourne ministry. In either case, Peel felt, the result would be a decline in popular respect for governmental authority, and the passage of a series of laws which would undermine both society and the constitution. This, he convincingly argued, was too high a price to pay for a brief period in power.

Support for Lord Melbourne only worked of course if the Whigs were resolute enough to remain in office. Once they were overwhelmed by their difficulties and decided to resign, Peel was placed in a new and more difficult situation. To refuse to form an administration would be irresponsible, but to head a minority ministry in troubled times would be to shoulder responsibilities without the means of discharging them. Either way unwelcome strains would be placed on the party at a time when its consolidation was incomplete. In December 1834 William IV dismissed the Melbourne ministry, which he did not like. His excuse was that the Prime Minister had expressed doubts on his government's ability to conduct business now that Althorp, the leader of the House of Commons, had been raised to the peerage on the death of his father. Wellington was sent for and was asked to form a ministry. He indicated that Peel would be a more suitable choice, and his advice was followed. It happened that the Conservative leader was wintering abroad, so there was a period of intense political speculation while a messenger hastened to Rome, and Peel, with wife and daughter, crossed Europe by coach, with hardly a break from the jolting and cold, in under a fortnight. Political gossips found much to amuse them while they waited in the activities of the Iron Duke who, taking things in his normal serious fashion, drove from department to department each day to transact the essential business of government single-handed. Peel had plenty of time to consider the political situation as he travelled. He quickly decided that circumstances made it impossible for him to refuse the King's commission, for the return of the Whigs to office only weeks after their dismissal would have turned William into their prisoner, unable to exercise his prerogative over the choice of ministers. Having taken this decision, which has been criticised as being based on an outdated view of the King's constitutional position, Peel seems to have forgotten the drawbacks of the situation, and to have allowed a sense of excitement to cloud his political judgement. Not only did he believe that Stanley and Graham, prominent Whigs who had recently resigned from the government, would join him, but he also felt that a majority in favour of his government would be returned in the event of a general election. Even when disappointed in both these respects, he continued in office in the belief that support would gradually rally round him as the parliamentary session progressed. He had at last, however, to recognise that his position was hopeless. In April 1835 he resigned.

Four years after his resignation, Peel was once again asked to become the head of a minority government, on Melbourne's departure from office in May 1839. The situation was not one to be relished, as Queen Victoria (who had succeeded in 1837) was openly sympathetic to the Whigs, and seemingly insoluble problems abounded in both foreign and domestic affairs. There appeared little to be gained and much to be lost by an assumption of power at this stage. Yet a refusal was out of the question, for it would have been construed as an admission on the part of the Conservatives that they were unfit to rule. Thus, as the lesser of two evils, Peel set about forming an administration. He hoped to strengthen his position by obtaining from the Queen some public indication of her approval, and decided to request the removal of several of the Ladies of the Bedchamber who were closely related to prominent Whigs. The Bedchamber Crisis followed, with Victoria resolutely defending her right to select her own household companions, and Peel maintaining that without a sign of royal favour his ministry could not continue. He did not, however, intend to allow the development of a constitutional crisis, and when Melbourne and his colleagues, flushed with notions of chivalrous conduct, proclaimed their determination to stand by their young Queen, he discreetly stood down in their favour. There can be no doubt that Peel acted as he did in part because he wished to spare Victoria, as woman and queen, from the public humiliation which would have resulted from any insistence on his claims. But he must also have felt relieved that the cup had been dashed from his lips. He much preferred the idea of assuming office with a majority behind him and with fewer major problems to be immediately faced. The problem of keeping the Whigs in power until he was ready to form a strong government was being solved for him. By June 1841, however, the fragile unity of the Whigs had been destroyed. Peel, feeling that his hour was nigh, proposed a vote of no confidence in the government. The ministers fought back energetically (even arranging for a certifiably mad supporter to be brought to Westminster) but without success. The motion was carried by one vote. The Whigs chose to dissolve Parliament rather than resign, but had miscalculated the mood of the country. The Conservatives secured a large majority (variously estimated at between 76 and 91) in an election said to have been a matter of 'Peel or not Peel'.

3 In office   When Peel became Prime Minister in September 1841 there was a general feeling of relief in political circles. This even extended to staunch supporters of the Whigs, many of whom had been made uneasy by their party's seeming inability to get to grips with the problems of the day. These, along with less committed men, were pleased that at last somebody worthy of trust and respect had taken up the reins of government. Seldom has a politician been the recipient of so much genuine and non-partisan support. Even after five years in power Peel had many devoted admirers, including Harriet Martineau, whose *History of the Thirty Years Peace* is full of praise for the minister and his measures. Several later historians have been as decided in their judgements, and have seen 1841-6 as a period of outstandingly good government.

There is much evidence for them to cite in support of their contention. In foreign affairs, along with his close friend Lord Aberdeen, the Foreign Secretary, Peel proved that it is possible for a great Power to be both respected and liked. By recognising that other countries had rights and feelings which could easily be ignored or hurt by such insensitive statesmen as Palmerston, he prepared the way for some sensible compromises and graceful gestures which created a fund of goodwill for his country, especially in France, without sacrificing one essential interest. A similar high-minded attitude was evident in Peel's handling of patronage. His ideas on the subject had already been formed when he was sent to Ireland as Chief Secretary in 1812, and he had caused a considerable stir by studiously refusing to appoint friends or relations to well-paid sinecure positions. As Prime Minister, he ensured that his colleagues understood his dislike of corruption, while he himself set a fine example by displaying a scrupulous regard for honesty in all things. He used his power of recommending the creation of peers sparingly, and then only in favour of men who had earned it by outstanding service to the state, and he granted pensions on the basis of public rather than of party merit. This was in contrast with earlier ministers who had taken it for granted that the ever-decreasing supply of patronage should be used to strengthen support for the government. Miss Ramsay claimed that 'more than any other individual man, Peel helped to raise the tone of political life', and this is true, especially as he left behind him a group of ardent disciples (such as Gladstone) who accepted and practised the principles of their master throughout their political careers. It should be remembered, however, that Peel was supported by the full force of public opinion, and that once he had decided to make a stand, his task was relatively easy.

Ireland is the best example of Peel's policy of making public appointments on the basis of justice. In this case, however, he was much more interested in treating the main religious groups fairly than in promoting individuals by merit. It was only after the passage of Catholic Emancipation in 1829 that the eighty per cent of Irishmen who were Catholics were eligible to hold most posts of official responsibility, and little had been done by the Whigs to correct the injustices of centuries, despite the efforts of Thomas Drummond, their Under-Secretary from 1835 to 1840, who had worked and worried himself into a premature grave. When Peel appointed Earl de Grey (who was no relation of Earl Grey, P.M. 1830-4) Lord Lieutenant of Ireland, he instructed him to go out of his way to give patronage to Catholics, and the same orders were given to his successor, Lord Heytesbury. More than this, Peel attempted to appoint a Catholic Under-Secretary of State for Ireland, but he was forced by his colleagues to realise that this would be taken as a major insult to the Protestant establishment. At least his motives were praiseworthy.

Peel's desire to have prominent Irish Catholic laymen placed in official positions was part of a wider strategy. He aimed to win over reasonable middle-class Catholics to support the existing constitutional relationship between England and Ireland, for he feared that in time of war an enemy might find in the Emerald Isle a discontented leadership capable of organising rebellion. He hoped that once inequalities based on religion were removed, propertied men of all creeds would unite together, and forget their poorer co-religionists. This process would be speeded up, he believed, if Protestant and Catholic could be educated in the same establishment. Therefore he insisted that the National Board, set up by the Whigs in 1831 to promote undenominational elementary education, should continue to receive state aid, although it had been catering almost exclusively for Protestants. While it existed there remained the hope that it would carry out its duties properly. Peel saw the possibility of doing more in the field of higher education, both to reduce bigotry and to provide more equal opportunities for rich Catholics. In 1844 he proposed the establishment of three Queen's Colleges, two of which would be destined for and controlled by Catholics, where an unprejudiced sectarian education would be provided. In addition, the existing college at Maynooth would be expanded so as to enable it to do more than train young Catholics for the priesthood. Peel's plans were assailed on all sides. The colleges were denounced as 'godless' by prominent Anglicans, and were opposed by the Catholic hierarchy in Ireland, who wished to keep the education of their young people in their own hands. Once the colleges were set up they were generally boycotted by Catholics, and in 1851 the Pope was prevailed upon to condemn them. Their impact was, therefore, much reduced. In England, however, the greatest stir was caused by the decision to increase Maynooth's annual grant from £9000 to £26,000 and to provide £30,000 for rebuilding. Hostile petitions arrived in their hundreds at

Westminster from all parts of the country, nearly a third of the Conservative backbenchers voted against the measure on its first reading, and Gladstone resigned from the Cabinet because he believed himself publicly committed to oppose state aid to any but the established Church. It is much to Peel's credit that he forced through what he considered to be beneficial legislation in the face of violent, if mistaken, opposition, which for a time seemed likely to destroy the unity of his party.

There were limits, however, to the equality which Peel was prepared to accord Catholics. He was worried by the fact that the wealthy established Church of Ireland served only ten per cent of the population, while the poor and non-established Catholic Church enjoyed the support of eight times as many, but he was unwilling to touch the wealth of the Anglican Church in Ireland, because he believed in the correctness of its dogma and the sanctity of property. One of the most divisive issues of the previous decade had been the appropriation of Irish Church moneys to lay purposes, and Peel's views were too decided for him to consider amending them. He was, however, increasingly prepared to grant the Catholic Church new rights which would make its inferior position less galling. He altered the law so that land could be bequeathed to the Catholic Church, and so that all Catholic bequests would be under the control of Catholics, and not Protestants as formerly. There is even strong evidence that in 1846 he wished to bring forward a Bill designed to end the penury of the Catholic priesthood by the use of government funds. Such a scheme would surely have been defeated, for none of the other churches would have accepted it, but it is illustrative of the lengths to which Peel was prepared to go in order to conciliate moderate Catholic opinion.

Halévy wrote that 'if there was a statesman . . . whose chief preoccupation was the material conditions in which the people lived, he was Sir Robert Peel, and everyone knew it'. Few historians would quarrel with the tenor of this statement. Equally, most would agree with Prince Albert that Peel's concern for the welfare of the people was 'passionate'—based on genuine feelings of sympathy rather than on an intellectual aversion to suffering. This he had proved in earlier years, when in 1818 as Chief Secretary for Ireland, and in 1826-9 as Home Secretary, he had been prepared to set aside his dislike of state-financed relief measures, which he labelled 'quackery', in order to curtail extreme suffering in famine-stricken and industrially depressed areas. The purity of his motives was shown by his insistence that the money should appear to come from either the King's private purse, or from an unknown source. While in office as Prime Minister, he was equally humane when in 1845-6 the potato blight brought famine conditions to parts of Ireland yet again. Believing that private enterprise could be relied upon to bring food to most areas, he concentrated on the problem of the remote districts. On his own initiative he ordered the purchase of maize worth £100,000 for sale in such places, which 'proved the decisive factor in relieving the distress of 1845-6', and encouraged the establishment of public works so that the destitute could earn money to buy food. Although the size of the disaster has made the government's actions seem inadequate to many, it is probably true that many of the Irish poor were better off in the summer of 1846 than in normal years.

Peel was wise enough, however, to realise that the disease of poverty would never be cured by treating the symptoms alone. Therefore, on coming to power in 1841, he searched hard for ways of dealing with the real cause, which he diagnosed to be the slackness of trade. The result was the budget of 1842, which is one of the financial landmarks of the nineteenth century. Peel was no more a doctrinaire free trader than Huskisson had been, but, like his former colleague, he believed in removing or lowering tariffs which hampered the country's trade. The Board of Trade had produced evidence in 1840 to bear out the contention of its permanent officials that most tariffs on raw materials raised the price of British manufactured goods, thus making them less competitive abroad, while doing little to increase the revenue, because the cost of collection was so high. They also claimed that no British industry, except for ship-building, silk-weaving and agriculture, had any need of protection from foreign competition. Peel was not totally convinced by their arguments, but he used them to help justify his decision to reduce or abolish more than three-quarters of the existing duties, so that no raw material was charged at more than 5 per cent, no semi-manufactured article at more than 12 per cent, and no manufactured goods at more than 20 per cent. His second great budget, of 1845, was equally effective in freeing trade, so that, in all, Peel abolished about two-thirds of the duties which had existed in 1841, including all export duties and most tariffs on raw materials. He hoped that this would lead to a greater demand for British goods and therefore to more regular and better-paid employment for the labouring classes so that they would be able to afford improved material conditions.

It is for the abolition of the duties on imported corn, however, that Peel is most famous, because his decision to repeal the Corn Laws, made between the summers of 1844 and 1845, admitted publicly in late 1845, and carried out in 1846, caused a political crisis of the first degree. Even before his conversion to repeal, however, Peel had significantly altered the corn duties by his budget of 1842. He took this action although he still believed that agriculture had special claims to protection on account of its heavy tax burden, dependence on good weather, and vital role in the nation's economy, because he saw that the existing sliding scale, which had been introduced by Wellington's ministry in 1828, was unsatisfactory. Not only did it cause bread to be unnecessarily expensive even after an average harvest, by placing a high tariff on foreign grain in such circumstances, but also it led to inflated prices in bad years, when importers waited for the official price of wheat to reach 73/- per quarter before releasing their stocks, so that a duty of only 1/- per quarter would be charged. Had they sold when the official price was 69/-, the duty would have been 16/8. Peel's new sliding scale tackled both these problems. By approximately halving the duty to be paid on imported wheat when the home price was between 52/- and 73/-, the law made it more likely that foreign grain would come on to the market as soon as prices exceeded the norm for the time of year; and by reducing the tariff, with two exceptions, by 1/- whenever the price rose by the same amount, the law made it less remunerative for merchants to hold on to their foreign supplies until prices rose. No longer was there a rapid reduction in the duty at the upper end of the scale. The same Act furthered the cause of imperial preference, towards which Peel was very sympathetic, by allowing Canadian grain to enter the country on payment of 1/- per quarter when home prices reached 58/-, rising to 5/- per quarter for prices below 55/-. Peel hoped that he had balanced the just claims of all parties. He claimed 'a sincere desire to afford to agriculture and the agricultural interest every protection which they could legitimately expect' as well as a desire to facilitate the entry of foreign corn whenever the interests of the consumer required it.

Although Peel was unprepared in 1842 to pledge himself to a policy of permanent agricultural protection, he did not imagine that in the immediate future circumstances would so alter that a tariff on corn would be unacceptable. And yet within three years he found that the arguments in favour of some measure of protection for British corn growers, which he had taken for granted for thirty years, were no longer convincing. Indeed he found himself unable to deny the validity of the free trade case. His position was especially difficult because he was the leader of a party which was popularly imagined to be wholeheartedly in favour of the Corn Laws, and which was kept in power by the votes of backbenchers many of whom had made promises on protection to their constituents in 1841. To add to this, the frequent parliamentary encounters on the subject, provoked by Cobden and Bright, made it impossible for the Prime Minister to remain neutral. Yet Peel's strategy, revealed to two close friends in the spring of 1845, depended on his conversion remaining a secret for twelve months, for he intended during the session of 1846 to 'confess that his opinions had changed, tell his party that he could no longer defend the Corn Laws, and, free from all obligations, . . . go to the country at the next election as a Free Trader'. Such a plan, which had much in common with that adopted by Gladstone after his conversion to Home Rule for Ireland, smacks of optimism rather than of practicality. Peel's attachment to the agricultural interest was already doubted by many who inferred the worst from his manufacturing background, the sliding scale of 1842, and his failure to use budgetary surpluses to reduce the tax burden of the farming community. A failure to speak in favour of the status quo in a whole year's Corn Law debates would not go unnoticed.

It is to be surmised, therefore, that Peel was relieved when the autumn of 1845 brought confirmation of a poor wheat harvest and a partial failure of the Irish potato crop, for at last the time of waiting and worrying was over. Urgent action was required if widespread and extreme hardship was to be avoided, and both Prime Minister and Home Secretary were convinced that the duties on grain must be suspended, so that stocks already held in bond at the ports could be released, and fresh supplies imported. For his part, however, Peel could not countenance a policy of deception. He was unprepared to ask Parliament to suspend the Corn Laws when such action would seem to promise a return to the existing system once the emergency was over, which was not his intention. The only honest course of action seemed to be to announce his conversion to his colleagues, and, should they support him, to promote in the Commons a Bill to repeal the Corn Laws. To resign on the grounds that his party was pledged to the protection of agriculture seemed to Peel to be selfish, for while resignation would safeguard honour and reputation, it would leave the country without strong leadership at a time of crisis, and would leave the starving at the mercy of the Whigs, whose leaders still, in October, were not in favour of Repeal. He presumed that he would be criticised for his decision, and he was. Not only political opponents of the time but also some historians have suggested that besides having erred in thinking that the end justifies the means, he was guilty of succumbing to a desire to remain in power or the compulsion to become a martyr. It is certain that writers will continue to argue over the motives of Peel for many years to come, as the evidence by its very nature cannot be conclusive. It has been said that 'motives are hidden in men's minds, and only God can disentangle them', but this should not discourage historians from attempting to explain why men act as they do, although it should warn them against claiming certainty for their theories.

On 31 October 1845 Peel asked the Cabinet to agree to an immediate opening of the ports and to the recall of Parliament so that a Bill to effect a lowering of the sliding scale could be introduced. That his startled colleagues, some of whom were markedly hostile to the aims of the Anti-Corn Law League, asked for time to think and did not at once declare against the proposals, suggests that Peel's moral authority over his Cabinet was considerable. This impression is strengthened by the way in which all but two of the Cabinet rallied to their leader and supported the amended proposals, providing for the extinction of the corn duties by stages over a period of three or four years, which he brought before them on 2 December. And yet the dissenting voices of Lord Stanley and the Duke of Buccleuch were sufficient to cause Peel to place his resignation in the hands of the Queen three days later.

No convincing explanation of this apparent loss of nerve has so far been forthcoming. It is clear that the support of Stanley and Buccleuch (although the former was a considerable speaker) was not vital and that their refusal to support Peel was the occasion rather than the cause of his resignation. Quite probably, the true cause was Peel's fear that he was acting wrongly in once again championing a measure which he had previously opposed. He seems to have been convinced that resignation was now his proper course, and he may well have promised himself that he would step down if he did not receive encouragement from all his colleagues. What confidence he had in his own decisions must have been undermined by the publication on 27 November of a letter from Lord John Russell, the Whig leader, to his constituents, in which he announced that he now favoured the total repeal of the Corn Laws. This destroyed Peel's conviction that he was the only man who could pass an essential piece of legislation: the Whigs now had to be taken into consideration.

On the resignation of the Conservative government, Victoria sent for Russell to ask him to form an administration. After travelling for six days and consulting for six days, Russell informed the Queen that he would be able to accept her commission, only to find within two days that he had misunderstood the terms on which some of his friends would serve. When Peel arrived at Windsor on 20 December in order officially to relinquish his offices, he was informed that Russell's attempts to form a government were at an end. This news seems to have destroyed his doubts and uncertainties, for on being asked to remain in office he replied, 'I want no consultation, no time for reflection. I will be your minister, happen what may. I will do without a colleague rather than leave you in this extremity.' Such impetuosity suggests Peel calmed his troubled conscience with a somewhat sentimental sense of chivalry. Just as the purposeless Melbourne found a fresh conviction in 1839 as a result of the appeals by his girl-Queen, so Peel in 1846 was able to persuade himself that a refusal to serve his still young, if matronly, monarch was out of the question. Perhaps self-deception was the only way out of a situation in which all possible courses of action were morally objectionable. Peel could now write, 'I feel like a man restored to life after his funeral service had been preached.'

Peel's new-found certainty infected his colleagues when he asked if they would serve with him. Wellington found it impossible to ignore the call to battle; the Prime Minister's old friends and young disciples showed more devotion than ever; and even Buccleuch was thrown into a confusion which prevented any immediate decision. Only Stanley could remain aloof from the spirit of comradeship which the meeting engendered. This personal triumph led Peel to minimise the hostility which he would encounter from his own backbenchers. He presumed that most would rally to him rather than force the destruction of the party. It soon became apparent that he was wrong when he stated his intentions to the Commons on 22 January. Both the extent and the asperity of the attacks launched by the Protectionists amazed him. At the end of February, 231 Conservatives voted against the second reading of the Corn Bill, while only 112 voted for it. But what surprised Peel more was the vigour of his opponents, which transformed what he imagined would be a short if bloody battle into a five months campaign. It was not until 28 June that the Bill passed its third reading in the Lords, and by that time Peel had been the recipient of more malicious criticism than he could ever have thought possible. The attacks were led by Benjamin Disraeli, who could hardly believe that fate had made so vulnerable the man who had refused to admit his suitability for office in 1841, and who since had done nothing to make good his mistake. He was aided by Lord George Bentinck, who, having previously hardly spoken in the Commons, became a national figure overnight because of his displays of hatred and contempt for Peel, the man who was disregarding the gentleman's code of honour. After this nobody could maintain the belief that the Conservatives were merely suffering internal disputes: they were a split party.

Because historians, especially during the late nineteenth century when free trade ideas were supreme, have claimed that the destruction of the Corn Laws was a major landmark in the economic history of this country, it is tempting to argue that Peel intended revolutionary change to follow. It has been said that he aimed to end the dominance of agriculture and instal industry in its place, or finally to break the power of the landed aristocracy, which had never fully accepted him, and to raise up merchants and manufacturers, whose origins he shared. It seems, in fact, that his intentions were less far-reaching. As with his other measures to remove restrictions on trade, he hoped that industry would be encouraged, and that the poor would receive the indirect, but real, benefit of regular and adequately rewarded work. But he had also come to realise—and this he claimed to be the basis of his conversion—that wage rates were not related to food prices, so that in times of scarcity the workers, even in the countryside, were condemned to greater suffering by the operation of the Corn Laws. It was mainly to lower the price of bread, the basic food of the English labouring poor, that Peel wished to repeal the Corn Laws. In his last words to Parliament as Prime Minister he foresaw that as a result of his Corn Act 'those whose lot it is to labour and earn their daily bread by the sweat of their brow' would be able to 'recruit their exhausted strength with abundant and untaxed food'.

In his speeches of 1846 Peel tried to persuade his listeners that he was not legislating against one section of the community and in favour of another. He stressed that his Corn Bill, which would leave a much reduced sliding scale in operation until 1849, after which a nominal duty of 1/- per quarter would be levied, was an act of justice, designed to end the situation in which an overwhelming majority of the population paid an unnaturally high price for grain so that the rent-rolls of landowners could be maintained. He claimed that the change was for the good of the country and not only in the interests of industry. So that the agricultural interest could not complain that it was being picked upon, a Customs Bill was passed at the same time. As a result of it, British manufacturers lost those remaining tariffs on manufactured goods which were considered to be protective, so that they, like the farmers, would have to face the full force of foreign competition. To prove further his contention that food producers deserved no special protection, Peel also passed a measure in 1846 which removed from the rural parishes a burden of taxation which landlords had used to justify their privileged economic position. No longer were Boards of Guardians in manufacturing districts to be allowed to send back to their place of birth, which was frequently rural, unemployed workers who applied for poor relief. Instead they were to care for those who had been living under their jurisdiction for five years or more. It was expected that this would produce a reduction of the poor rate in much of the countryside.

Perhaps the most praised feature of Conservative government, 1841-6, was the restoration of the nation's finances. Nothing had done more to undermine the public's confidence in the

Whigs than the successive deficits of their last five years in office. Year after year they had failed to balance income and expenditure, so that when the financial year 1841-2 produced a deficit of more than £2¼ million, the total deficit for recent years approached £8 million. The measure of Peel's success is that for all but his first year in office he returned substantial surpluses, while managing to remit many taxes, paying off £14 million of the National Debt, and reducing the rate of interest payable on another £250 million of it. The contrast of before and after could hardly have been clearer. This miracle was only possible because Peel was prepared to reintroduce the hated income tax which the younger Pitt had first levied. Even at the rate of 7d. in the £ on incomes over £150 p.a. the new tax yielded £5 million, or 10% of the government's needs, and thus both covered any natural deficit and allowed many imposts to be lowered or abolished. The tax also had the pleasant side effect of reducing the proportion of revenue contributed by the working classes, for with weekly incomes rarely exceeding 35/- even skilled men were exempt. Peel did not, however, introduce this measure in the pursuit of social justice. He intended it to be no more than a stop-gap until trade quickened, when it would be dispensed with. Little did he imagine that a tax, approved in 1842 for a period of three years and renewed for the same period in 1845 in order to allow the tariff reductions of that year would have a continuous life of more than 130 years. Nor could he have expected that its introduction would be met with so little hostile comment. In fact the informed public had for some time realised that only novel procedures would correct a situation which Whig tinkering had made worse. Similarly, Peel's decision of 1842 to renew the existing Poor Law for a period of five years generally accepted in Parliament, even by those Conservatives who had taken up the anti-Poor Law cry at the general election the year before. People were prepared to take from a minister they trusted much that they would have objected to if brought in by the former administration.

This confidence in Peel was the result of men's belief that he would do everything possible to preserve the essential structure of society. Their trust was not misplaced, because at a time when continental observers were predicting a cataclysmic social upheaval for Britain, the Prime Minister was determined to curb the excesses of popular agitation, while legislating where permissible to cure the economic malaise which fed discontent. In contrast with the seeming weakness of the Whigs when faced by the Chartist challenge of 1838-9, Peel's reaction to the troubles of 1842 was positive and determined: and when O'Connell's agitation in Ireland reached alarming proportions in the summer of 1843, there was no retreat at the threat of civil war as there had been in 1829 over Catholic emancipation. But Peel did more than maintain law and order, for he was determined to strengthen the nation's economy so that 'thoughts of the dissolution of our institutions should be forgotten in the midst of physical enjoyment'. It is for this reason that historians have considered the budgets of 1842-6 to be so vital a part of the Conservatives' claim to have provided England with good government.

Few writers have had anything but praise for the measures that have been described. There are some matters, however, about which opinion has been sharply divided. The Bank Charter Act of 1844 was designed primarily to control the amount of paper money in circulation. It limited country banks to the totals they had then issued, and the Bank of England to £14 million plus the value of bullion held by the Issue Department, which was rigidly separated from the Banking Department. The fact that this system remained in operation until well into the twentieth century, and thus served Britain throughout its period of world economic domination, has led some historians to claim that the Act was responsible for the sound monetary system which the country enjoyed. Even those who do not go so far have tended to give Peel general praise for his measure, at least on the ground that it was lasting. But even granted that Peel understood the limitations of his Bill and realised that in times of crisis it might have to be suspended, as it was in 1847, 1858 and 1866, it is difficult not to be critical. Such a rigid limitation of credit as that envisaged by the Act would have strangled the economy had it been enforced, but fortunately Peel had overlooked the fact that other forms of credit, such as cheques and bills of exchange, played an important part in commercial life. Equally the splitting up of the Bank of England into two un-coordinated departments was damaging in that it reduced flexibility. Perhaps it is unfair to say that the financial system worked well despite the Bank Charter Act, for it ended the granting of unrealistic amounts of credit by small banks which had been largely responsible for the crisis of 1836-7, but it is true that the success of the Act was somewhat fortuitous, and as such should not redound to the glory of Peel or the Bank of England officials whose advice he followed.

If the tendency has been to overrate Peel's reform of the banking system, the opposite has happened with his interest in the reform of factories. This has largely come about because writers have approached the subject from the standpoint of ardent campaigners such as Lord Ashley, the later Lord Shaftesbury, who were far from satisfied with Peel's attitude. Using such sources as the letters and diaries of these men it has been possible to come to the conclusion that Peel was the 'chief obstacle' to legislation in favour of factory workers. The lukewarm support given by Peel to the Mines Act of 1842, which made it illegal for boys under ten and all females to work underground, his refusal to challenge the Lords when they substantially modified the Bill, and his repeated opposition to the introduction of the ten-hour day, have all been quoted to strengthen the case. But this interpretation is too one-sided. While it is true that in 1844, after a large number of Conservatives had voted against their leader and in favour of a ten-hours amendment, Peel used the threat of resignation to frustrate the efforts of the reformers, and that he was still against the measure when it became law in 1847, it is not accurate to say that he was generally uninterested in improvements in working conditions. The Mines Act received little of his attention because it did not require it, and the coal-owner peers were allowed to get away with their amendments because he gave priority to his belief that the upper House should retain its 'independence'. Despite this, he shared the public's concern over the sufferings of miners and was disappointed that political realities allowed so little to be done. Equally he was saddened by the long hours endured by factory workers, although he toiled longer himself, but was of the opinion that any reduction in hours must lower a standard of living which was already hardly tolerable. He presumed that shorter hours must lead either to a reduction in wages or to a decline in profits, which would encourage manufacturers to invest their capital elsewhere in the hope of higher returns, thus putting many of their hands out of work. He had no doubt that by voting against attempts to lay down a maximum ten-hour day he was acting in the interests of the working classes as well as of the country.

He was, however, far from believing that nothing could be done, for from 1842 he was working with Sir James Graham, the Home Secretary, on a measure to improve the Factory Act of 1833. The effort to provide schools so that the education of factory children, legislated for in 1833, could become more than a formality, was abandoned in 1843 when Nonconformists raised a storm over the plan to place the intended factory schools under the control of the Church of England, but useful improvements were made. The Factory Act of 1844 permitted children to work a maximum of $6\frac{1}{2}$ hours per day, instead of 9, and for the first time restricted the hours of women to 12 per day, forbade those covered by the Act to clean moving machinery and insisted that machines be fenced in. Peel was aware, however, that his legislation affected only a small proportion of the working community, for it did nothing for those employed in non-textile factories, workshops or their own homes. He hoped that public opinion, aroused by the official reports on conditions, which he encouraged, would force employers to improve the conditions of those whom he felt the law could never be made to reach. In fact, his hopes were no better founded than his opinion that it was impossible for the state to regulate all places of employment. This does not mean, however, that his sympathies were not genuine or his achievements negligible.

While Peel has often been congratulated on his efforts to win over the Catholics of Ireland, he has also been accused of failing to tackle the country's land problem in a determined way. Cecil Woodham-Smith has written that until the famine he 'continued to contemplate the condition of the Irish people with imperturbable apathy'. His critics have, however, generally overrated what it was possible for him to do and underrated what he was willing to do. No popularly elected politician can be expected to go against the basic values of his society, and it is unreasonable to blame Peel for refusing to launch the comprehensive attack on the rights of property which would have been necessary to solve Ireland's interrelated problems of absentee landlords, middlemen, sub-division of holdings, high rents, insecurity of tenure and old-fashioned farming methods. Given the power structure of the time, no British statesman could have carried out the fundamental reorganisation that was required. Peel was aware of the seriousness of the situation and of his powerlessness to deal with it. He was therefore once more forced to hope that if he focused public attention on the problem, landlords with the power to effect changes would do so. Thus in 1844 he set up a Royal Commission under Lord Devon to inquire into the relations between landlord and tenant in Ireland, and by appointing able and eminent men to serve on it, ensured that its findings, which were published in 1845, would be taken seriously. This was made more certain by the speed with which the government attempted to put into effect one of the Commission's recommendations. The Tenants' Compensation Bill of 1845 was the first measure introduced by a British government to improve the position of the Irish peasant in respect to his landlord. That it would have done no more than erect a somewhat cumbersome procedure by which evicted tenants could receive compensation for three types of improvements, even had it become law, should not be allowed to obscure the fact that the Bill attempted to modify the rights of property owners. It has been argued that had Peel remained in power for several years more he would have carried the process further, and so earned the praise of posterity.

It is not possible to speak well of all the actions of Peel's administration. The way in which O'Connell's trial was managed after his arrest in October 1843 is especially worthy of censure. Peel and his colleagues realised that their subordinates in Ireland were making a mockery of justice by their insistence on a Protestant jury, a partisan judge and fabricated charges, but seem to have been willing to countenance such proceedings in order to secure a conviction. Some would accept that at certain times an individual must be sacrificed for the good of the state, but none have accepted that the situation in 1844 required it. By that time the agitation of the previous year had died down, and the real challenge to the government had ended. The fact that English public opinion, normally so hostile to O'Connell, was outraged by the treatment he received suggests that the government had been guilty of more than an error of judgement. At no other time was Peel's integrity so open to question, but on occasions he did act unwisely. His appointment of Lord de Grey as Lord Lieutenant of Ireland was in many ways most unfortunate, for a man less willing to appoint Catholics to government posts could hardly be found. Thus Peel found himself with a head of the Irish establishment who would not implement the government's policy, a situation which was made worse by the Prime Minister's reluctance to bring pressure to bear. As a result, little could be done towards winning over moderate Catholic opinion until ill health forced Earl de Grey's retirement in 1844. Equally unwise was Peel's handling of the Church of Scotland, many of whose members had come to dislike the power enjoyed by lay patrons over the appointment of ministers. When in 1842 church leaders of this persuasion attempted to take the law into their own hands, Peel, determining that legality must be maintained, adopted an uncompromising attitude, with the result that in the following year one half of the members of the Church of Scotland seceded to form the Free Church. One can feel sympathy for Peel, as for George III in his struggle with the American colonists: both had right on their side and yet failed in their efforts to force their opponents to be reasonable. But one must admit that he failed to understand that a fervour based on principle rather than on interest is not stilled by harsh words. By his firm stand he precipitated the secession, whereas a conciliatory approach might well have secured the unity that he desired.

4 Success or failure? On 29 June 1846 Peel resigned as Prime Minister because the previous day a number of his former supporters had joined with the Whigs to defeat the government over a Coercion Bill for Ireland. The issue had not been important to the Protectionists, but some of them had determined to destroy the leader who had betrayed them. This they did, for Peel never regained his fighting spirit, and having made the decision never again to hold office, he stuck to it. For four years, until his death in 1850, he remained in the Commons, a politician without a future, embarrassed by the devotion of former colleagues who felt unable to desert him. It is true that he had gone out with a bang rather than with a whimper, but there were many who found him a figure worthy of their pity. It seemed that he had failed.

An Emile Zola or a Thomas Hardy would be needed to do justice to the story of the man who laboured for years to construct a new party from the ruins of the old, only to sacrifice its unity in the mistaken belief that the interests of his country required it. Few, perhaps, would accept this as the story of Sir Robert Peel, although Disraeli's biographer, Monypenny, believed that Peel 'sacrificed his pledges and his party to a supposed necessity that had no existence', but there is something tragic in the way he brought about his own downfall by breaking up the party he had created. In the 1830s he aimed to build around himself a Conservative party which would be dedicated to strong government and the maintenance of the country's institutions, while accepting moderate measures of reform. By 1841 he had been so successful that he was able to form a majority government, and put his theories into practice. Through four sessions of Parliament he struggled to educate and discipline his followers. He achieved much, but then risked all by expecting them to sacrifice both principle and interest at the same time. Two-thirds rebelled, and the Conservative party dissolved into Peelites and Protectionists. In Ashley's words, Peel had 'reduced Parliament, party, and men's minds to original chaos'. There followed twenty years of 'the confusion of parties' during which two-party politics, re-established by Peel, was submerged. It seemed that all that had been done had been undone.

Opinions must always differ on the question whether Peel made the correct choice. It is possible to be sympathetic to the judgement of Disraeli that 'the first duty of an English minister is to be faithful to his party, and that good and honourable government in this country is not only consistent with that tie, but in reality mainly dependent on its sacred observance'. It is almost impossible to sustain democracy in a large country without a stable party system, as numerous states have found to their cost, and a stable party system cannot exist where leaders take it upon themselves to make fundamental policy decisions which seem to contradict the basic philosophy of the party without the agreement of a majority of their supporters. It could be argued that Peel risked doing more damage to his country by upsetting its delicately balanced political system than he could have done good by repealing the Corn Laws.

Those who applaud Peel's action normally do so in the belief that a politician should follow the dictates of his conscience whatever the consequences. The idealist, saddened by the selfishness of man, is heartened to find someone prepared to commit political suicide for the sake of justice. But one must beware the temptation to build up Peel as a paragon of virtue. He was not 'the noblest figure of his time' nor 'the politician who had no thought of self', and even Ashley was wrong to imagine that 'he will never do a dishonourable thing'. He was, however, a man who at certain times in his career found it possible to lay aside his great and obvious worldly ambition, though perhaps not his desire 'for a niche in history', in order to do what he believed to be right. The world is full of men who can fight to the top, and of those who will gladly give up whatever they have, but the man able to do both is a rarity.

There are valid reasons for judging Peel to have been a successful as well as a good man. The way in which he breathed new life into the Tory party, twice split in 1827 and 1829 and demoralised by the Reform Crisis of 1830-2, was a considerable achievement. But of greater significance for the country was the part he played in the struggle to prevent the break-up of society under the stress of economic and political change. To *The Times* obituary writer it was obvious that 'Peel has been our chief guide from the confusions and darkness that hung around the beginning of this century to the comparatively quiet haven in which we are now [in 1850] embayed'. It had been Peel's aim to convince the reactionary elements that change must come if a bloody revolution was to be avoided, and in this he was successful, for even those who fought to maintain the Corn Laws were soon to realise that it was unwise to go against the spirit of the times. Equally he wished to ensure that the supporters of rapid change should not be allowed to panic Parliament into hasty action or to organise a successful uprising, and his firmness and confidence contributed much towards the victory of law and order over anarchy and violence. Most important in this field, however, was the way in which he provided a rallying-point for moderates of all backgrounds, for in so doing he made certain that the voice of educated reason would be heard when decisions of vital importance were being made.

It has often been stated that Peel was forced to be a teacher rather than a prophet, as the bread-and-butter problems with which he had to deal were little suited to the exercise of high ideals or the exposition of general theories. Yet in one respect at least he managed to free himself from the immediate and the mundane in order to proclaim the gospel in which he believed. His greatest success was in attracting a band of disciples who would both practise and preach that gospel after his death, and make certain that the creed of government in the interests of the whole community became one of the basic standards of Victorian political life. To Peel good government meant many things. It required that those in power tackled their work with a seriousness that approached a sense of mission, for without it the government would be unable to play its part in the advance of progress; it required of a minister a devotion that left little time free for family or social life, and a capacity for sustained hard work which is not commonly found. For Peel this meant at one extreme that the business of every department, including the Foreign Office, had to be closely watched by the Prime Minister, a task which it was fast becoming impossible for any one man to carry out, and at the other extreme that every letter from a person of any importance had to be answered by himself. He also felt that to govern well it was necessary for the politician to be unselfish and to put the interests of his country before those of self, family, friends and party at all times, but especially when decisions on policy and patronage were being made. Considerable sacrifices could be required, and Peel allowed personal honour, family fortune, lifelong friendships and party unity to be damaged or destroyed for the sake of his country. Good government also meant moderation, with common sense rather than dogma as the basis of decisions; friends said this showed realism, but enemies claimed that it displayed opportunism or even a lack of principle. Peel popularised his ideas by practising them and by showing that they worked. His generation benefited directly from his actions, and succeeding generations have enjoyed the fruits of a tradition which he largely established. It is little wonder that Peel is considered to be one of the most important British politicians of the nineteenth century.

Chapter IV

O'Connell and Ireland

1 The problem In April 1829 Daniel O'Connell won his greatest victory, when the British Parliament sitting at Westminster passed an Act which allowed Roman Catholics to hold nearly every high civil and military office, including that of Member of Parliament. Catholic emancipation had come. Although many Englishmen had favoured such a measure for many years, they had been unable to overcome the opposition of the monarch and the House of Lords until O'Connell had stirred up the peasantry of Ireland and faced the government with the possibility of civil war. O'Connell, the highly successful Catholic barrister, born into the family of a clan chieftain from County Kerry on the Atlantic coast of Ireland, had won through where many others, including the younger Pitt, had failed. He was now often known as 'the Liberator'.

Yet even in his hour of triumph O'Connell realised that the problem of Ireland had only just begun to be solved, for the removal of political disabilities from Catholics had not ended the injustices suffered by the people of Ireland either as Catholics or as Irish. To O'Connell, the heart of the problem was that England still treated Ireland as she had been treated for over six hundred years, as a conquered land. No longer, as in the sixteenth and seventeenth centuries, were marauding armies sent to terrorise the natives, or landowners dispossessed so that Englishmen could enjoy their revenues or Protestant Scots be settled on their estates, or penal laws passed in the hope of reducing all Catholics to a state of uneducated and poverty-stricken savagery, but equality was still a long way off. The eighty per cent of Irishmen who were Catholics had little opportunity to take part in the administration of their country, because the British government chose to maintain and to rule through the Protestant ascendancy. Ever since the Battle of the Boyne in 1690, when the Catholic army of James II had been defeated by the Protestant followers of William III, Catholics in Ireland had been regarded as potential traitors and excluded from positions of responsibility. Even after emancipation had come in 1829 it required great courage for a British government to appoint a Catholic to an important position in the central government of Ireland, based, under the Lord Lieutenant, on Dublin Castle. On the whole it seemed safest and wisest to continue as before, relying on the closed corporations monopolised by Protestants to control the towns, the Anglo-Irish Protestant landowners as magistrates to control the countryside, the all-Protestant Royal Irish Constabulary, backed up by non-Irish army units, to protect lives and property, and a Protestant bench to punish wrongdoers, their hands strengthened by Coercion Acts which allowed arrest and imprisonment without trial in times of emergency. The election of a number of Catholic M.P.s and the appointment of a number of Catholics as J.P.s and a few as K.C.s did not constitute the collapse of the Protestant ascendancy.

In religious as in governmental matters not all Irishmen were treated equally. The church of a small minority, the Protestant Church of England and Ireland, was recognised by the state as the established church and enjoyed vast revenues from church lands and tithe, while the church of the large majority, the Church of Rome, had no official position and subsisted on the contributions of its members. England too, of course, had its established and non-established churches, but there the situation was made less intolerable by the fact that the established church was not only the largest but was also a genuinely national church having its origins in the history of the country and fulfilling a vital role in most communities. In Ireland the established church was another aspect of the Protestant ascendancy, a symbol of conquest, confiscation and subjection. It had been imposed on the people, and had found no place for itself in the lives of many towns and villages, where the Catholic priest had for centuries been the most important figure.

Although the Protestant ascendancy in all its forms was anathema to O'Connell, he reserved the full force of his fury for the way Ireland was governed from Westminster. He considered it to be his country's gravest misfortune that decisions concerning its welfare were made hundreds of miles away by a parliament largely ignorant of or uninterested in the problems that were particular to Ireland. He believed Ireland to be at the mercy of English politicians who, regarding the country as a burdensome problem, either ignored the situation, legislated without any real understanding of what was at stake, or, worst of all, gave in to pressure from powerful British interests and passed laws which were harmful to the Irish.

To the modern historian it is obvious that Ireland's major problem was neither political nor religious, but economic. In the 1830s it would have been difficult to find elsewhere in Europe such extensive misery and degradation, where a quarter of the population was without work for a large part of the year, where more than half the people came near to starvation in the summer months of most years, and where the most common type of dwelling was a single-roomed mud hut without windows, and most probably without furniture. The conditions of the rural Irish, of course, had never been good, but during the eighteenth century and early decades of the nineteenth what seems to have been an almost unparalleled increase in population, without a corresponding increase of productive capacity, imposed fresh strains on the economy. Although there is insufficient evidence to speak with certainty, it seems likely that the population of Ireland rose from something over three million in the 1770s to about eight million at the time of emancipation. There was no industrial revolution to provide work for the extra hands, as there was in England, for the country lacked raw materials, political stability, and, outside Ulster, a suitably prepared industrial base from which to expand. The effect of British competition, long seen by Irish nationalists as the major cause of their country's industrial impotence, is a subject on which historians fail to agree, for the surviving evidence appears to support contradictory interpretations. At the same time the acreage of land under cultivation failed to increase adequately because both landlords, many of whom lived in England, and tenants, most of whom had no legal safeguard against eviction at short notice, were unprepared or unable to invest the necessary money or energy in the drainage of untilled land. Thus in many villages extra mouths had to be fed from the existing fields; fathers divided their already meagre holdings between their grown sons; many families had insufficient land to grow a whole year's supply of potatoes; increased competition for land led to increased rents; and everywhere poor people were having to survive on less and less. Worst of all, in many parts of Ireland, especially on the west coast, dependence on the potato had become complete. In good years the crop was sufficient to feed the family, provide seed for the next planting, and allow some to be marketed to provide money for essential expenditure; in less good years, with fear for the future ensuring that seed potatoes and rent money remained intact, extremes of hunger became commonplace. Who could doubt what would happen should there be a very bad year?

2 The ideal solution   Until 1800 College Green, Dublin, was the home of a separate Irish parliament. In that year the younger Pitt, anxious to bind Ireland more tightly to Britain in order to reduce the likelihood of another insurrection inspired, assisted or dominated by the French, such as that of 1798, persuaded the parliaments of Dublin and Westminster to pass an Act of Union, stating that from 1 January 1801 there would be but one parliament for the United Kingdom of Great Britain and Ireland. It would meet at Westminster, and would contain representatives of the Irish peerage, as well as one hundred commoners representing Irish constituencies. Money, places and honours had had to be liberally distributed to secure the assent of the all-Protestant Irish parliament to the measure.

What to Pitt had been the marriage of two nations was to O'Connell the rape of one by the other, and from the very beginning he had opposed it. During all the years he agitated for emancipation he was certain that all would not be well with Ireland until her parliament was returned to her. He struggled meanwhile to bring about the less important reform because he realised that the chances of obtaining Catholic emancipation were much greater than those of effecting the repeal of the Act of Union. As a realist he had to admit that whereas English opinion was sharply divided over the emancipation question, it was united in a desire to maintain the Union. None the less he rarely doubted that Repeal was the ideal solution to Ireland's problem. This did not mean that he wished to see Ireland established as an independent state: rather he desired that within the framework of the United Kingdom matters of concern to Ireland should be decided by Irishmen in Ireland.

O'Connell, like the Chartists, believed that the people would not be well governed until they had control of their own affairs. He frequently told his audiences that the reforms that Ireland so urgently required would only be passed when there was once again a parliament on College Green. Then changes would be made which could never attract majority support in an assembly dominated by Englishmen. As the *Nation* newspaper, in the years after 1842 a most respected voice of Irish nationalism, put it, 'Repeal would abolish absenteeism and foreign taxation, and would give Irish offices and rewards to Irishmen . . . would secure the peasant from oppression, the mechanic from premature competition, and, with justice, would bring order, industry and riches.' Repeal to O'Connell and his followers, however, was more than a key to good government, it was a symbol of Ireland's nationhood. While the Union endured, Ireland was very much the junior parnter and Irishmen were no more than rather inferior Englishmen. National pride demanded the restoration of ancient rights, with their implied parity of esteem. Perhaps Dublin, as a city, had never been the equal of London, but it was clear that since 1800 it had been dying. The people of Ireland gladly believed that a restored parliament would give their capital new life.

Harriet Martineau stated that in the 1830s and 1840s O'Connell neither wanted nor expected to obtain Repeal. While it seems unreasonable to question his desire for a return to the situation before the Union, it may be that only when he was carried away by his own eloquence did he genuinely believe that Repeal would come in his own lifetime. Certainly he always showed himself willing to lay aside his grander claims in order to obtain a measure of reform for his country, and in contrast to the leaders of Chartism and the Anti-Corn Law League, was able to say, 'I am always for taking an instalment when I cannot get the whole.' Thus in his quieter moments he seems to have decided that although Repeal was what Ireland really needed, good government from Westminster was more likely to be secured and would serve almost as well. When the Whigs came to power in 1830 with a determination to reform Parliament, it seemed to O'Connell that the time was drawing near when a fair and sympathetic treatment of Ireland's claims might be expected. He could therefore hope for legislative action to cure some of his country's ills, especially those concerned with religion and politics. It was to be expected that the Whigs, with their traditional links with Nonconformity and religious toleration, would not look kindly on the established church in Ireland with its unnecessarily large income, in part derived from tithes, a tax on agricultural produce paid by the grower and collected by proctors who were hated for their objectionable methods. Also O'Connell could hope that a reforming government would sweep away the undemocratic borough corporations and replace them with elected councils on which Catholics would have an opportunity to serve, as well as giving to Ireland the extra parliamentary representation that her population warranted, and repealing the law of 1829, which had changed the voting qualification in Irish county elections from a 40/- to a £10 freehold while leaving the British franchise as before.

O'Connell spoke and wrote less about Ireland's economic problems than he did about matters of principle which involved justice and right. This is not surprising in a man who, having grown up where riches amongst poverty were accepted, had found that the poor would rather be taken out of themselves and their suffering than be reminded of it. It does not mean, however, that O'Connell was unaware that a problem existed. Rather, as a landowner who took it for granted that property rights should be protected and not invaded by the state, and as a follower of the political economists who did much to spread the creed of *laissez-faire*, he doubted whether legislation was an appropriate way to tackle economic ills. The nearest to an ideal solution he was prepared to support was compensation for improvements, twenty-one year leases for all tenants-at-will, and a tax on the rents of absentee landlords.

3 Ways and means   Addressing a crowd of supporters from the balcony of his Dublin home in December 1830 O'Connell proclaimed, 'I told you that if you took my advice, we would achieve emancipation. Did I deceive you? Let me tell you now that if you take my advice you will repeal the Union.' But within weeks the government's determination to prevent the growth of a fresh agitation in Ireland, indicated by the banning of each new organisation O'Connell founded, brought home to the Liberator what he must already have known, that the time was not ripe for an attempt to destroy the Union. For the next decade he largely confined talk of Repeal to the hustings at election times, and only once, under pressure from his followers in April 1834, brought the subject to the notice of Parliament. The result, after five days of debate, must have convinced all concerned of the futility of such action: only one English member joined with thirty-seven Repealers from Ireland to vote against more than five hundred who wished to maintain the Union. O'Connell was now well placed to persuade his 'tail', as critics derisively termed the thirty to forty members who generally accepted his leadership, that the only practical aim was good government for Ireland within the existing system. The fact that a Whig ministry favourable to reform rather than a Tory ministry was in power added attraction to such a policy.

O'Connell's method of extracting concessions from the government altered as experience taught him the limitations of his power. Between the end of 1830 and the end of 1834 he acted as the leader of a completely independent party, refusing to accept high legal office from the Whigs for fear that it would impose restrictions on his freedom. He gave the government open support when it took action of which he approved, but denounced it in extreme terms when it failed to do all he considered necessary. He presumed that the strength of his denunciations would convince the Whigs that it was wise to buy his silence by doing as he wished over Ireland. He was wrong because the government, and especially Stanley (Chief Secretary for Ireland, 1830-3), was angered by his attacks and became all the more certain that it was senseless to risk losing English support in order to gain that of Ireland. Peel's minority ministry of 1834-5 and the general election of 1835 led both sides to reconsider their tactics. The Whigs, realising that the 1832 Reform Act had not guaranteed them a future of large parliamentary majorities, became aware that the support of the Irish Repealers was important, and perhaps vital, while O'Connell, horrified at the prospect of a lengthy term of office for his arch-enemy Peel, and conscious that he had achieved little since 1829, decided that attacks on the Whigs would do little good but might do much harm. The result of these changes in attitude was the Lichfield House Compact of 1835, an unwritten agreement between O'Connell and the Whigs to unite together to overthrow Peel, which led to five years of very close co-operation. O'Connell surprised his allies by showing that he understood the delicacy of their situation. He gave the Whigs regular support in return for no more than the promise that they would do what they could after consultation with him to secure whatever Irish appointments and legislation seemed suitable. He surrendered his freedom of action without insisting on office for himself or the implementation of particular detailed policies. This straightforward relationship lasted until O'Connell was reluctantly forced to admit in 1840 that Melbourne and his colleagues were doing less than they reasonably could. Then, to stimulate the Whigs to take steps to remedy Ireland's remaining ills, he recommenced the agitation for Repeal, although without confidence that his action would do more than further undermine an already dispirited ministry. In 1841 the Whigs, in the hope of strengthening their position, called a general election and were defeated.

The victory of the Conservatives meant to O'Connell that there would no longer be a government with which he could co-operate, for throughout his political career he had identified Peel and his party with the Protestant ascendancy. Thus with no alternative that would satisfy his conscience, O'Connell was forced to face up to the ultimate question whether or not to go for Repeal. Even at the age of 66 he could not contemplate withdrawing from public life while the possibility remained of achieving his life-long ambition, so he decided that his Loyal National Repeal Association must become the main object of his attention.

As O'Connell thought out the campaign which he hoped would end in Repeal, he was certain of one thing above all else: he would never countenance the use of physical force. As a young man he had been sufficiently distressed by the excesses of the French Revolution and the aftermath of the rebellion of 1798 to be determined that he would never be the cause of such sufferings. Thus the methods open to him were somewhat limited, especially as his legal experience had impressed upon him the necessity of always acting within the law. It is not surprising, therefore, that he should have fallen back on the technique which had proved so effective in the 1820s, the mobilisation of the masses.

Whereas the Chartists and the Anti-Corn Law League experienced difficulties in finding good leaders in many localities, O'Connell was able to call upon an efficient existing organisation, the Catholic Church. Not only did he have the support of the majority of the bishops, but—of more importance—he could rely on the good offices of the bulk of the parish clergy. It was the word of the priests that made it possible for a branch of the Repeal Association to be founded in almost every village. And it was the priest who normally appointed a trusted parishioner to act as Repeal Warden to organise activities within the community. The most important of the warden's duties was the collection of the Repeal Rent, a contribution of $\frac{1}{4}$d per week made by each member to the Association's funds, but it was also hoped that he would stir up enthusiasm, especially by holding meetings and establishing a reading room where such periodicals as the *Nation* would be available.

But O'Connell did not rely entirely on local initiative to build up the agitation. Under friends and relations a staff of full-time workers was employed in Dublin, ensuring that branches were not left without advice, and that speeches by O'Connell and his lieutenants were well publicised. In the summer and autumn of 1843 a series of some forty monster meetings was organised throughout the length and breadth of Ireland, normally held on a Sunday afternoon and followed up by a banquet for the more wealthy supporters in the evening. Hundreds of thousands attended each of the large meetings, and even those who were unable to get within range of O'Connell's stentorian voice seem to have been impressed by the sight of him speaking.

In 1842 O'Connell said, 'Let me have Repeal Wardens in every parish, and my plan is complete and success is certain.' One must clearly not take at face value all that popular leaders say in order to boost the morale of their supporters, but O'Connell's actions show that he believed that the existence of three million Repealers in Ireland would have a profound effect upon Peel and his colleagues. Like the Chartists with their petitions, he seemed to imagine that governments listened to the clearly expressed will of the people. Certainly he planned his monster meetings in part to show the government how united Ireland was in its wish for Repeal. Yet although he had 'an exaggerated faith in the efficacy of constitutional methods of agitation', he was astute enough to realise the value of an implied threat. He was not prepared to be an O'Connor (whom he despised as a lapsed disciple), bluffing about civil war, although he did become sufficiently excited at one meeting to declare, 'The time is come when we must be doing . . . you may soon have the alternative to live as slaves or die as freemen', but he was only too keen to draw Peel's attention to the obvious fact that the people of Ireland, once aroused, might be unwilling to follow his counsels of moderation. He hoped that Peel would be sufficiently frightened to give way as he had done in 1829.

O'Connell did not use only the spectre of rebellion to put pressure on the government; he was equally prepared to imply that unless Ireland were granted the legal right to rule herself properly, she would seize it for herself. When, in May 1843, twenty-four magistrates had their commissions withdrawn for having attended Repeal meetings, a system of arbitration courts, modelled on those set up by rebels in Canada a few years previously, was established. They were officered by respected gentlemen of Repeal sympathies, and handled civil cases where both parties agreed to be bound by the court's decision. Their success surprised many people and did much to raise the spirits of Repealers. Their main purpose, however, was to warn the government that a united people could ignore the organs of an unsympathetic state. The same message was inherent in O'Connell's promise of 1843 that he would soon summon a Council of Three Hundred to meet at College Green in order to discuss the affairs of Ireland. He intended that Peel, fearing that control was slipping out of his hands, should graciously grant what he saw he could not withhold.

4 The course of events O'Connell's victory in the County Clare by-election of 1828 had been planned as a challenge to the government over Catholic disabilities, rather than as the commencement of a parliamentary career. None the less, after being put to the trouble of a second election by the Protestant diehards in Parliament who insisted that the Catholic Relief Act should be worded so as to nullify the result of his first contest, O'Connell took his seat at Westminster in February 1830. Such a decision was not taken lightly, for attendance at the Commons would make it impossible for him to continue his legal work on the scale necessary to provide him with a gentleman's income. A remarkable solution to the problem was found by his devoted friend, Fitzpatrick, who organised the continuation of the Catholic Rent as a fund for O'Connell's personal use. In an average week several hundred thousand Irishmen paid $\frac{1}{4}$d so that their Liberator could continue to represent them, while living in the style that his position demanded.

That O'Connell failed to make as much impact on Parliament as people had expected is not surprising, for he was now uncertain how to win over an educated and hostile audience ill-attuned to the flattery and vulgarity which were so effective in Ireland. Soon, however, he found a hopeful cause to work for when the Whigs introduced their First Reform Bill in March 1831. For the next fifteen months he strove to secure radical changes in the electoral system, but was most disappointed in the final Acts, especially that for Ireland, which increased the country's representation by only five seats, left many of the borough constituencies in the hands of Protestants, and maintained the hated £10 freehold qualification for voting in county elections. His disillusionment deepened when he realised that the reformed parliament which first met in 1833 was no more inclined than its predecessor had been to give serious consideration to the question of Repeal, and that the Whigs had no intention of giving the Radicals a strong and enlightened lead. Not only did they pass a Coercion Act in 1833, granting wide-ranging powers to the Irish authorities, in an effort to overcome the refusal of most Catholic tenants to pay their tithes, instead of taking action to do away with what O'Connell felt to be an unjustified burden on his co-religionists, but they also gave in to the Tory peers and abandoned their plan, detailed in clause 147 of the 1833 Irish Church Bill, to devote some of the funds of the established church to secular purposes. This to O'Connell was betrayal, although the Act suppressed ten sees and taxed stipends of more than £200 in order to raise money for the repair of churches so that the Church Cess, an unpopular rate previously used for that purpose, and payable by landholders of all religions, could be abolished. A greater betrayal, however, was yet to come in the following year, when Littleton, the Irish Secretary, having promised O'Connell that in return for the withdrawal of the Repeal candidate from the Wexford by-election the clauses in the Coercion Act relating to courts-martial and the banning of public meetings would not be renewed, asked the Commons to continue the Act in its original form. O'Connell's anger was unrestrained, and his denunciation of the government's bad faith provoked a crisis which ended in Grey's resignation and his replacement by Melbourne as Prime Minister.

Despite the generally poor relations between O'Connell and the Whigs, 1832-4, there followed a period of what seemed to contemporaries dishonourably close co-operation. O'Connell abstained from all agitation in favour of Repeal, exerted his influence in Ireland in favour of peace and good order, and helped out the government when its existence was endangered by the defection of its more radical back-benchers, while the Whigs, for their part, tackled those of Ireland's problems which were considered amenable to legislative action, and attempted to follow the dictates of liberty and justice in their administration of the country. The question of Irish tithes was never allowed to be long forgotten, for violence frequently accompanied attempts to enforce the law, especially early in the decade when some tithe proctors were 'dragged from their beds, and laid in a ditch to have their ears cut off'. The Tithe Composition Act of 1832 had done a little to improve the situation by making it compulsory, instead of voluntary as it had been since 1823, to establish the tithe as a fixed cash payment rather than as a payment in kind varying with the size of the crop, and by making the last lessor rather than the occupier responsible for payment. In this way the number of people from whom tithe was to be collected was drastically reduced, and the haggling over it avoided. But a satisfactory solution remained to be found. O'Connell was prepared to accept the government's Bill of 1835 which would have transferred responsibility for payment to the landlord, at a rate 25 per cent lower than that at the time prevailing, although Catholic tenants would still have been supporting an alien church through increased rent charges, because it was planned to appropriate to educational purposes the tithe from the 860 parishes with fewer than fifty Church of Ireland members. The House of Lords, however, stood firm against the confiscation of church revenues and the Bill was defeated in 1835, 1836 and 1837. Only in 1838, when both the Whigs and O'Connell had had plenty of time to realise that an Act without appropriation was better than no Act at all, were the Lords' terms accepted and the Bill passed.

The Whigs intended to replace the generally corrupt and Tory-dominated corporations of both English and Irish towns with a system of democratic local government, but the Lords, forced by the strength of domestic public opinion to allow the passage in 1835 of the Municipal Corporations Act, dealing with England, were determined to save the Irish boroughs from the clutches of a Catholic shopocracy. Under the influence of Lord Lyndhurst they not only defeated government Bills in 1836 and 1837, but also asserted their independence by refusing to accept what was virtually an agreed measure between Peel and Russell, the leaders of the two main parties in the Commons, in 1838 and 1839. Only when all their major objections had been met was an Act reforming the Irish corporations passed in 1840. Once again O'Connell was pleased to accept something rather than nothing, even though in the ten of the fifty-eight old corporate boroughs which were to retain a council election would be by freemen, most of whom were Protestants, and £10 householders, thus excluding the poorer and overwhelmingly Catholic ratepayers. It was a bitter pill to swallow.

Whereas England had been blessed with a Poor Law system since the sixteenth century, the poor of Ireland had always been forced to rely on friends and relatives or the charity of rich men when personal, regional or national disasters struck. The Whigs thought it should be otherwise, and were supported by many property holders in England who felt that Ireland should care for its own destitute rather than encourage them to cross the water and become a burden to the British ratepayer. O'Connell was torn many ways, for whereas he favoured dispensing with a Poor Law system, the majority of his followers wished there to be outdoor relief, and the government introduced a Bill to establish a system of the English type in Ireland. In the end he decided to oppose the Bill, but it became law in 1838.

Although the Lords could frustrate the Whigs' attempts to pass laws in the interests of Ireland, they could not affect the way in which the country was administered. Here at least the government could implement its good intentions. Great care was taken over the making of appointments, both large and small, for not only was O'Connell's advice or acceptance normally sought over important ones, but under Thomas Drummond (Under-Secretary 1835-40) minor ones also received considerable attention. Especially significant was the way in which Catholics were enrolled in the Royal Irish Constabulary, and chosen to serve on juries, in an effort to breed in a new generation of the poor a respect for the law, which was generally looked upon as a tool of British oppression. The impartiality of the administration was further publicised by the suppression of Orangemen's lodges, which were the Protestant equivalent of the banned Catholic associations, and by Drummond's controversial reminder to landlords that they had duties as well as rights. Perhaps most pleasing to liberal-minded men, however, was the way the Whigs managed to rule Ireland during Melbourne's second ministry using only the normal legal processes. No new Coercion Act was passed and the existing one was not put into effect. It is no wonder that O'Connell hesitated to commence a fresh agitation when the Whigs seemed to be proving that good government could come out of England.

Nevertheless the Precursor Society was founded in 1838, its name a clear warning to the government that although its aim was not Repeal it would become a more extreme organisation unless more was done for Ireland. O'Connell decided two years later that the time for a renewed agitation had come, and an association which was later to become the Loyal National Repeal Association was launched. At first, however, the signs were not encouraging, for despite a considerable effort to obtain a large attendance only one hundred came to the inaugural meeting in Dublin. Of those only fifteen were prepared to join.

The reason was no mystery, for many doubted whether O'Connell was in earnest, while others were unprepared to go as far as Repeal, and it was only slowly that the new movement gathered momentum. It was not helped by the fact that many of the trusted helpers of Catholic Association days had grown old or respectable, with no new generation trained to take their places, nor by O'Connell giving up a whole year of his time to being the first Catholic Lord Mayor of Dublin.

Historians have dated the coming to life of the Repeal agitation from various events in late 1842 and early 1843. Unfortunately the surviving evidence is not sufficiently representative for us to be able to judge their relative importance in stimulating support for the movement, although it is clear that they all played a significant part. The establishment of the *Nation* newspaper in October 1842 not only gave some able young men the opportunity to use their talents to the full in the cause of Repeal, but also made it possible for the fires of nationalism to be rekindled in the hearts of tens of thousands of Irishmen, both rich and poor. On the last day of February 1843 O'Connell gave a brilliant oration lasting more than four hours before the Dublin Corporation in support of a motion favouring Repeal, which was widely reported and received great public acclaim, especially because of the convincing arguments it contained. In April the first monster meeting was held and the process whereby millions of ordinary Irishmen were to experience the emotional and corporate attraction of the Repeal agitation was under way. In May the dismissal of twenty-four Catholic magistrates, including O'Connell and Lord ffrench, on account of their Repeal activities resulted in large numbers of well-to-do and moderate men joining the Repeal Association.

If several factors were responsible for launching the movement into popularity, one above all caused it to grow to such an extent that Graham, the Home Secretary, became convinced that a civil war was about to break out, while Peel himself was not prepared to discount the possibility. The forty monster meetings, attended by crowds which made all but the largest

Chartist gatherings of 1838-9 seem insignificant, created a unity of feeling which had rarely been equalled in Ireland's history. Its extent can be diagnosed from the size of the weekly totals of the 'Repeal Rent', which rose from £60 early in the year, through spring figures of £700, to more than £2000 at the end of May and a maximum of £3103 7s 6½d in mid June. By late summer O'Connell was at the head of a mass movement before which he believed the government must bow, if only to the extent of offering concessions such as a subordinate parliament to sit in Dublin, or legislation to make the local government and electoral systems of Ireland as democratic as those of England.

Peel and his colleagues, however, were determined not to be intimidated, having announced in May that the Union would be maintained even at the cost of civil war. Several policies were considered, but in the absence of Cabinet unity no action was taken until a mistake on the part of the Repealers allowed those who favoured punitive measures to gain the ascendancy in early October. O'Connell planned to make the last monster meeting of the season a fitting climax to the year's work, and it was decided to hold it at Clontarf, outside Dublin, the site of Brian Boru's historic victory over the Norsemen. In O'Connell's absence a poster, couched in military terms, was published to explain the arrangements for the meeting, and this, although hastily withdrawn, gave the government the legal right to ban the gathering. Peel, listening to those who wished to make the Irish leader pay for his effrontery in challenging the declared will of Parliament, and to Graham who believed that unless O'Connell was brought down he would be forced to progress to unconstitutional and possibly violent action, sent Earl de Grey back to Ireland to stop the meeting and to arrange for the arrest of all the important Repeal leaders. The fact that the proclamation banning the meeting was only issued at 3 p.m. on Saturday, 7 October, after many of the people intending to be present at Clontarf the next day had already set out on their journey, has given rise to some strange theories. Some Irish commentators have considered it to be proof of the government's desire to provoke a breach of the law so that troops could be used to shoot down unarmed peasants and thus put an end to the agitation, while some admirers of Peel have claimed that he displayed consumate political skill in allowing the Repealers so little time for an organised reaction. The truth, however, is much less revealing: the proclamation came so late because the timing of the government's decision and the initial failure of the Dublin authorities to use the correct legal phrasing allowed it to come no sooner.

The banning of the Clontarf meeting was the great crisis point in O'Connell's career, for it faced him with a terrible dilemma. He had either to comply with the proclamation and risk losing the support of the masses to whom he had promised early successes and pledged resistance should the government interfere with the right of peaceful assembly, or he must carry on with the meeting and, acting illegally, make bloodshed, if not civil war, a certainty. In the event O'Connell's decision was immediate, for not only had 'fear of violence and disorder become an obsession with him', but his common sense told him that, given the moral power and military strength of the government, nothing could be achieved by a peasant rabble however determined it might be. He cancelled the meeting and did all he could to ensure that a quiet Sunday followed.

Thereafter O'Connell was a spent force, not because his followers deserted him, for his arrest a week later, his trial and sentence of a year's imprisonment in February, and his unexpected release in September 1844, all helped to make him more popular, but because his sense of purpose had left him. While most historians have agreed that after 1843 O'Connell was a changed man, they have differed in their explanations of why it was so. Most common has been the assertion that he became increasingly mentally unbalanced, and although the evidence is not sufficient to convince all his biographers, his unrealistic passion for a young woman two generations his junior, the emotional devastation caused by the death of a favourite grandchild, and at the end his strange fear that he would be buried alive, are all indicative of a mind that could no longer keep events in their true perspective. Even before 1843 political gossips hawked the supposed fact that O'Connell feared prison more than anything else, and there were those in the government who advocated using the threat of arrest in order to cure the Repeal fever. Certainly his actions during the months between his initial arrest and his trial suggest that there was substance in the rumours, for he tried distastefully hard to create an image of himself as a calm and law-abiding citizen. One should not forget, however, that victim of madness or cowardice as he may have been, he was also an old man who had been forced to admit that his policy was bankrupt, that 'he had called out the people, and now did not know what to do with them'. The aged must not be expected to show the resilience of youth.

Between his release from prison and his death while on a pilgrimage to Rome in May 1847, O'Connell resumed his political life, but to no good effect. Instead of capitalizing on the government's embarrassment at the Law Lords' decision to reverse the verdict of his trial, he allowed the mass agitation to die away while toying with schemes such as federalism which he believed the Whigs might be induced to support. His inaction, along with his refusal to listen to the advice of others than old friends and his son John, exasperated the faction within the Association known as Young Ireland, which had always disliked his dependence on Catholicism, his playing down of cultural nationalism, and his refusal to sanction the use of violence. In June 1846 the Young Irelanders, further disgusted by O'Connell's decision to commit his parliamentary following to the support of Russell's newly formed Whig government, left the Repeal Association, but showed little ability to organise or to agree among themselves and achieved little more than a comic opera rising in Tipperary in 1848. In the same year the Repeal Association, lacking real leadership and clear objectives, dissolved itself.

5 Success or failure? O'Connell was probably a more controversial figure than any other politician of his time, and since his death the debate has continued. With notable exceptions opinion has been markedly hostile, which is not surprising since most of his biographers have been either Irish or English. Although they have named their most famous street after him, the Irish do not look upon O'Connell as a great hero: they save their praise for those who achieved more. Sir James O'Connor in his *History of Ireland* published less than fifty years ago stated, 'The highest claim that can be made for O'Connell is that he antedated Emancipation by a decade.' While few have judged his achievements so harshly, many have pointed out that the period of co-operation with the Whigs yielded little of value to Ireland; there were unsatisfactory solutions to the problems of tithe, poverty and urban government, and the beginnings of good government were not built upon. More strikingly, however, it has often been claimed that whereas O'Connell did little good, he did much harm. The later writings of the stalwarts of Young Ireland, especially Sir Charles Gavan Duffy and John Mitchel, have been largely responsible for this tradition. Duffy felt that O'Connell was guilty of 'misleading and betraying the Irish people in 1843' and that by so doing he 'destroyed the Repeal movement at the summit of its influence and demoralised the Irish masses'. More comprehensively, Mitchel wrote that O'Connell led Ireland 'all wrong for forty years'. Such critics, including more recent Irish writers who regard as heroes the men of the Easter Rising of 1916, blame O'Connell for failing to employ the only tactics which would have righted Ireland's wrongs in the 1840s—armed rebellion. They find especially sickening the thought that more than a million died as a result of Britain's inaction during the Famine, while O'Connell refused to sacrifice a few thousand lives to free Ireland from such barbaric government. Even before O'Connell died, Ireland's economic problems had been forced into the limelight, where they were to remain for the rest of the century. Thus some historians have been perplexed by O'Connell's seeming indifference to the sufferings which have since become a part of the country's folk heritage, and have accused him of acting in the interests of his own landlord class. At best he has been blamed for failing to understand the true needs of Ireland

English writers have also had every temptation to treat O'Connell with scant sympathy. Not only has he been suspect on account of his Catholicism, especially in the nineteenth century, when 'no popery' sentiments were still widespread even in educated Protestant circles, but his aims have also made Englishmen classify him as one of their country's enemies, thus making it more difficult for them to assess his career in a non-partisan way. Most of all, however, his character and temperament were not of the type which generations of Britons have come to expect from their public men, and the criticisms of English writers have largely resulted from this. The basis of Harriet Martineau's contempt for him, which pervades the pages of her history, was his provision of 'repeated proofs of his utter unworthiness of all trust', while *The Times* felt justified in describing O'Connell as

> Scum condensed of Irish bog,
> Ruffian, coward, demagogue,
> Boundless liar, base detractor,
> Nurse of murders, treason's factor.

In particular his management of financial affairs has earned him the condemnation of many Englishmen, brought up to believe that it is acceptable to dispense charity but not to receive it. It was well known that throughout his parliamentary career he relied on the 'tribute' from Ireland to maintain his solvency, and many have echoed the sentiments of Disraeli, who wrote scornfully of his 'princely revenue, arising from a starving race of fanatical slaves'. Equally, the fact that he was a demagogue, stirring the emotions of gathered multitudes, offended the Englishman's sense of decorum, for even as late as 1880 it was considered uncouth of Gladstone to go on a speaking tour. Such beliefs have since died out, but it is still possible to criticise O'Connell for being a rabble-rouser. 'Swaggering Dan' was a nickname employed by those who did not approve of his flamboyance in word and action, which they termed vulgarity. Certainly he enjoyed showing that he was 'an artist in vituperation', for, as the *Annual Register* of 1838 termed it, he was 'conspicuous for the loose and exuberant impetuosity of his tongue'. England, with its tradition of tolerance and moderation, has rarely in recent times looked kindly on exponents of extreme abuse.

On the continent of Europe, however, O'Connell has frequently found favour as a great champion of personal and national liberties. Balzac rated him as one of the three greatest men of the nineteenth century, and the Belgian rebels of 1830 thought him fitted to be their king. Even in England some have considered him quite outstanding. Gladstone called him 'the greatest popular leader whom the world had ever seen'. Certainly as the creator of modern Irish nationalism he is a figure of great importance. Even if his rousing of Ireland almost single-handed in the 1820s brought forward the passage of Catholic emancipation by only a few years, it also established a tradition of political action on a national scale which he could himself draw on in the 1840s and which made the task of Parnell so much easier forty years later. It may, however, be that 'his real influence was much more moral than political', for his campaigns did much to promote in a peasantry which had been downtrodden and dejected for generations a sense of national pride and a hope for better things in the future. He restored a degree of self-respect to those whom poverty had robbed of more than material prosperity. As with the Chartists, however, it is impossible to produce quantitative evidence to support such a judgement: one can merely refer to the general statements of contemporary witnesses and one's 'feel' for the period.

Not all O'Connell's achievements were so intangible, for his agitation of 1843 seems to have had a real political impact. Peel was very forcibly reminded that immediate action was required to solve Ireland's problems, and the result was the enlightened policy which he pursued until the end of his ministry. Had it not been for the Famine, which overshadowed the reforms preceding it, O'Connell's achievement might have been more obvious. As it was he left Ireland with her major problems unsolved. He failed to do for his country all that he wished, but he probably achieved as much as could have been expected given the political system and climate of the time, and his own belief that the end does not justify the means. His limitations were obvious but so were his strengths. It is difficult not to warm to a man who devoted so much of his life to the cause he believed in and who refused to sacrifice others in a bid to achieve success. Perhaps he was right to believe that 'no human revolution is worth the effusion of one single drop of blood'.

Date Chart

1829 Catholic emancipation

Nov. 1830 Earl Grey's Whig ministry replaces the Duke of Wellington's Tory ministry

1832 First Reform Act

1834 Poor Law Amendment Act

July-Dec. 1834 Lord Melbourne's first ministry

Dec. 1834-April 1835 Sir Robert Peel's first ministry

1835 Tamworth Manifesto; Lichfield House Compact

April 1835-Sept. 1841 Lord Melbourne's second ministry

1836 London Working Men's Association founded

1837 Victoria becomes queen

1838 People's Charter made public; Manchester Anti-Corn Law Association founded

1839 First Chartist Petition; Bedchamber Crisis; Anti-Corn Law League founded

Sept. 1841-July 1846 Sir Robert Peel's second ministry

1841 Richard Cobden elected M.P. for Stockport

1842 Second Chartist Petition; Peel's famous budget

1843 Monster meetings in Ireland

1844 Trial and imprisonment of Daniel O'Connell; Bank Charter Act

1845 Partial failure of Irish potato crop

1846 Repeal of the Corn Laws

July 1846-Feb. 1852 Lord John Russell's first ministry

1847 Feargus O'Connor elected M.P. for Nottingham

1848 Third Chartist Petition

Further Reading

The most useful single-volume textbooks covering the period are Sir Llewellyn Woodward, *The Age of Reform 1815-1870* (O.U.P., 2nd edition, 1962) and Asa Briggs, *The Age of Improvement 1783-1867* (Longmans, 1959). Elie Halévy's unfinished *History of the English People in the Nineteenth Century* is very valuable, especially to those studying beyond 'A' level. The relevant volumes are *The Triumph of Reform 1830-1841* (Benn, 1950) and *Victorian Years 1841-1895* (Benn, 1951).

J. T. Ward (Ed.), *Popular Movements c. 1830-1850* (Macmillan, 1970) has chapters on Chartism, the agitation against the corn laws, and the Irish agitation. In the absence of a modern history of Chartism the best general account is M. Hovell, *The Chartist Movement* (Manchester University Press, 1918), although a fairly full picture can be obtained from the very readable G. D. H. Cole, *Chartist Portraits* (Macmillan, 1941). Asa Briggs (Ed.), *Chartist Studies* (Macmillan, 1959) is a collection of essays on particular aspects of the movement best suited to an undergraduate audience, as are F. C. Mather, *Chartism* (Historical Association, 1965), J. Saville, *Ernest Jones: Chartist* (Lawrence & Wishart, 1952), A. R. Schoyen, *The Chartist Challenge* (Heinemann, 1958), Read and Glasgow, *Feargus O'Connor* (Arnold, 1961). and I. Prothero, *Chartism in London* (Past & Present no. 44). H. T. Gaitskell, *Chartism* (Longmans, 1929) is an introduction to the subject by one who admits his reliance on the work of G. D. H. Cole. R. G. Gammage, *History of the Chartist Movement 1837-54* (2nd edition, 1894) and T. Carlyle. *Chartism* (1839) and *Past and Present* (1843) contain many interesting judgements and anecdotes.

N. McCord, *The Anti-Corn Law League* (Allen & Unwin, 1958) is the best book on its subject. D. G. Barnes, *History of the English Corn Laws* (Routledge, 1930) shows the movement in its full historical context. C. R. Fay, *The Corn Laws and Social England* (C.U.P., 1952) includes speeches by Peel on the corn laws. D. Read, *Cobden and Bright* (Arnold, 1967) examines the League's two most famous leaders.

No recent biography of Peel deals with the period after 1830 A. A. W. Ramsay, *Sir Robert Peel* (Constable, 1928) is a most interesting study, written in a lively and challenging manner. G. Kitson Clark, *Peel and the Conservative Party* (Bell, 1929) and N. Gash, *Reaction and Reconstruction in English Politics* (O.U.P., 1965) are valuable on Peel in opposition to those studying beyond 'A' level.

A. Macintyre, *The Liberator, Daniel O'Connell and the Irish Party 1830-1847* (Hamish Hamilton, 1965) and K. B. Nowlan, *The Politics of Repeal* (Routledge, 1965) are detailed accounts of O'Connell's later career. L. J. McCaffrey, *Daniel O'Connell*, (University of Kentucky Press, 1966) is a study of the events of 1843. C. Woodham-Smith, *The Great Hunger: Ireland 1845-1849* (Hamish Hamilton, 1962) contains in its early chapters a clear account of the problems of Ireland.

G. M. Young, *Victorian England, Portrait of an Age* (O.U.P., 1936) and G. Kitson Clark, *The Making of Victorian England* (Methuen, 1962) are very important books, essential to those wishing to acquire a deep understanding of Victorian England.

Index